SPIRITUAL TRANSFORMATION

THROUGH THE EFFECTUAL AND FERVENT PRAYER

TOM TIRIVANGANI

SPIRITUAL TRANSFORMATION

Published by
Tom Tirivangani Press and Publications
200 Sanford Ave North, Hamilton, Ontario
Canada L8L5Z8

Copyright © 2023 by Tom Tirivangani
All rights reserved. All rights reserved.
No part of this publication may be reproduced, stored in a retrieval system, or transmitted in any form or by any means except in the case of a brief quotation printed in articles or reviews without prior permission in writing from the publisher

First Printing, 2023

Contents

1	LET'S START FROM THE BEGINNING	2
2	WITNESSING AND SEEING THE REALITY OF THE POWER OF THE GOSPEL	13
3	THE FOUNDATION OF TRUE PRAYER	23
4	A RETURN TO THE TRUE GOSPEL: BRINGING CHRIST'S LIFE TO THE CHRISTIAN COMMUNITY IN THE LAST DAYS	27
5	BUT WHAT IS THE GOSPEL IN A NUTSHELL	40
6	EFFECTIVE PRAYER BY LEARNING TO TRUST GOD	48
7	TRUE PRAYER	54
8	WORDS OF WISDOM	58
9	UNLOCKING THE SECRET OF A SUCCESSFULL PRAYER LIFE	63
10	IMPARTATION OF THE SPIRIT OF PRAYER	72

Profound Heavenly Thoughts

"Confess your trespasses to one another and pray for one another, that you may be healed. The effective, fervent prayer of a righteous man avails much."

Elijah was a man with a nature like ours and he prayed earnestly that it would not rain, and it did not rain on the land for three years and six months. And he prayed again and the heaven gave rain and the earth produced its fruit - James 5:16-18

Chapter 1

LET'S START FROM THE BEGINNING

"He who has never learned to obey cannot be a good commander." Aristotle

It seems strange to start a discourse on prayer by looking at and examining a quotation from Aristotle's philosophical musings. In his book Metaphysics Aristotle tried to discuss the discipline of prayer.

In my theological understanding, reflection, and analysis Aristotle came to a very shallow projection and articulation of what Prayer is and what Prayer is capable of achieving. Maybe some of the readers are wondering who is Aristotle? Why does his view of Prayer matter? Aristotle is regarded as a philosophical genius of antiquity. His ideas have had a huge influence on many aspects of human life and thought for centuries. He is regarded as a legend in philosophy and a must-read for everyone who is going through a university education.

However, in my close examination of Aristotle's writings, I concluded that there is no evidence that Aristotle believed in the efficacy of prayer, that is there is God who is capable of hearing and responding to our prayers. Aristotle explicitly rejected prayer but thought that prayer could be useful in some other aspects of human life.

While Prayer seems very common and simple, yet in my study and examination of Prayer, I have come to the understanding that Prayer is a very complex discipline, whose functionality and purpose have been easily overlooked and glossed over by many people and is seldom understood.

Let me venture to look at the story of Albert Einstein, one of the world's most renowned Physicists as I continue to discuss the discipline of Prayer. His attempt to deal with the subject of Prayer shows a serious ignorance among the so-called educated, brilliant, and intellectual minds in history. They start from the wrong premise. Prayer can be talked about by almost anybody and many people suggest that they pray. Although prayer could be a subject of intellectual debate and discourse, prayer is much more complex.

PRAYER is a spiritual activity and can only be correctly understood with the help of the Spirit of God. To understand prayer in any other way will lead to futility and vain talk. "What we have received is not the spirit of the world but the Spirit that is from God, so that we may understand what God has freely given us. This is what we speak not in words taught by human wisdom but in words taught by the Spirit explaining spiritual realities with spiritually taught words. The person without the Spirit (of God) does not accept the things that come from the Spirit of God but considers them foolishness and cannot understand them because they discerned only through the Spirit" *(I Corinthians 2: 12-14).*

In Romans 8:26 Apostle Paul, a remarkable and renowned man of God makes a clear and profound statement; that Prayer is a Spiritual Activity and can only be understood through the Spirit of God and can also ONLY be accurately undertaken if it is done through the Spirit of God. Put simply Prayer is not an intellectual matter and must not be inoculated by the virtues of intellectualism and human philosophy. To do so is to mislocate and dislocate prayer and ultimately to pollute and adulterate it by subjecting it to an inferior form of human understanding.

I will go back and narrate the story of Albert Einstein as narrated in the book, "Dear Professor Einstein: Albert Einstein's Letters to and from Children," edited by Alice Calaprice, as reported by the Huffington Post. A sixth grader from a Sunday school at The Riverside church wrote a letter to Albert Einstein asking if scientists do pray. The young girl named Phyllis wrote this inquisitive note to the great Physicist and was surprised to receive a considerable reply. He replied a mere five days later on January 24, 1936, sharing his thoughts on science and faith. He said that scientists believe that every occurrence including the affairs of human beings is due to the laws of nature. Therefore a scientist cannot be inclined to believe that the course of events can be influenced by prayer; *that is by a supernaturally manifested wish.* However, he said that we must concede that our actual knowledge of these forces is imperfect so that in the end the belief in the existence of the final ultimate spirit rests on a kind of faith.

Such belief remains widespread even with the current achievements in science. But he also said that everyone who is seriously involved in the pursuit of science becomes convinced that some spirit is manifest in the laws of the universe, *"one that is vastly superior to that of man."* In this context Albert Einstein concedes that it is impossible to undertake any serious scientific inquiry without admitting that there is God who holds the galaxies together and science will not make any meaningful science until it admits that it is impossible to explain the metaphysical world without admitting that there is an uncreated being outside Matter, that is the subject of inquiry. How can I talk about the existence of the planets without seriously considering how those planets came into being? Who is the source? That source cannot be comprehended fully by human logic, and it seems and is indeed far beyond the scope of human logic and comprehension. How can the creature be able to describe fully and adequately the CREATOR? The lesser cannot fully comprehend the greater. This has been the error of science for centuries. This is the flaw of science, Matter is not the subject of science but of the Creator.

Prayer is the most wonderful thing I have ever encountered in spiritual my life and walk. Never has there been an experience that I have come across that can compare to a life of prayer. Prayer is talking to God, whom by his grace and mercy we call him "Abba Father". In Psalm 2: 7-8, David said *"I will declare the LORD's decree, He said to me: "You are my son today I have become your father. Ask me and I will make the nations your inheritance, the ends of the earth your possession."* God is our own Father. He acknowledges us as his own. In other words, we are not illegitimate children. Through Christ Jesus, who died on the Cross of Calvary 2022 years ago, we were brought near and received the adoption into sonship unto GOD, through the shedding of the blood of Jesus Christ.

We were ingrafted into the family of God, because of our faith in Jesus Christ. "Yet all who believed in His name, he has given the right to become children of God, not born by the will of man but born of God" (John 1:12). We became God's own special people. *"But you are a chosen people, a royal priesthood, a holy nation, God's special possession, that, you declare the praises of him who called you out of darkness into his wonderful light. Once you were not a people but now you are a people of God, once you did not receive mercy but now you have received mercy"* – 1 Peter 2: 9-10. Therefore, we are no longer foreigners to the Commonwealth of Israel. However, this can only be discovered when one studies the word of God and engages in deep and genuine prayer.

Prayer to me is a dynamic and powerful tool in the hands of a believer in Christ Jesus. To those who truly love prayer, being in prayer, I mean practicing prayer is like being emersed in fragrance. The purity, beauty, and the power of it is indescribable. On another hand, prayer can be a taxing and challenging experience. No wonder why I say, "Prayer is work but prayer works". I see prayer as real work, an output of an enterprise.

Prayer at a deeper personal spiritual level and reflection means the desire to work on oneself, to work on your character, and to work on your attitude consistently until Christ is fully formed in you. You work yourself until you come to the unity of faith and the knowledge of the son of God and you have become mature by attaining the full measure of the stature of Christ.

Apostle Paul, an imminent theologian, and scholar, an apostle with veritable marks of apostleship, demanded as he was writing to the Philippian church, *that each one must work out his or her salvation with fear and trembling.* Listening to the advice of Apostle Paul and reflecting on his teaching in his Pauline epistles, **Prayer is paramount**. It is only prayer mixed with faith and reading the word of God that can achieve that Spiritual transformation in a person's life. It is impossible to have a fully transformed Christian life without spending considerable time in meditation, fasting, and prayer.

For more than twenty years now I have soaked myself in prayer. I cannot start a day without prayer. Prayer has started to flow out of my life as a natural phenomenon. Prayer has become an integral part of my life. I have learned many ways of praying and have prayed many prayers that have lasted at times hours, weeks, or months. I mean praying a structured and organized prayer, with a specific agenda and an expected outcome.

I have learned to pray without ceasing. There are times I have locked myself in my office for two weeks, without coming out or talking to anyone but ONLY God. I have fasted for six months, continuously seeking the face of God. This has never been my personal power but the grace of God. This is truly nothing but the grace of God and therefore, there is no room for boasting.

I love to write about what I do. I hate to sit down and write about things or on a subject of what I've heard from people. I know there are many authors who wrote or write on prayer, but they do not pray. They have an intellectual knowledge of prayer. Our bookstores are full of books from such kinds of authors. My writing on prayer is inspired and experiential. I do not just write because I have knowledge of a subject. I cannot begin or dare to start unless the Spirit of God prompts me. When I sit down to write, God must inspire me. The putting of pen and paper together is an ACT of the prompting of the

Holy Spirit. In the practice of prayer, I have helped thousands of people jumpstart their prayer life. I am deeply convicted that prayer is the KEY that unlocks closed doors.

Prayer changes everything and changes everyone. I have encountered and have had the practical experience of the power of prayer. I have seen prayer working firsthand.

During my ministry, I have prayed for many people, and they have experienced miraculous manifestations of the power of God through prayer. Some who had cancer got instantly healed, and others who were seeking the fruit of the womb or had been barren for many years were released and have conceived children. Others were healed of mental illness and diabetes, some received financial breakthroughs, restoration, and the list goes on. I have seen the Power of prayer. Undoubtedly, prayer is NECESSARY. However, at this stage of my spiritual life, it is not just about praying for the sake of it. I am now more concerned about whether my prayer is being effective. I am now concerned about how much my prayer is helping me in building an effective and intimate relationship with God. I want to impact and impart the gift and Spirit of prayer to others. I am hungry to see God revive nations and the world through the ministry of prayer. But my prayer cannot have an impact on others until it has touched and changed me.

Properly handled prayer can birth wonderful and beautiful things if it is offered from a pure and clean heart and in faith in God. In this book, I will share with you the wonderful mysteries of God that can only be revealed through prayer. *"It is the glory of God to conceal a matter and the glory of kings to search it out."* (Proverbs 25:2). In my quest to know God better and develop an intimate relationship with Christ, I am by the grace of God seeking to know the hidden things of the

Kingdom of God. *"The secret things belong to the LORD our God, but the things revealed belong to us and to our children forever, so that we may follow all the words of this law."*(Deuteronomy 29:29). *Abraham believed God and it was accredited to him as righteousness.* (Genesis 15:6).

We now can hear God, testifying when he was about to destroy Sodom and Gomorrah, saying, *"When the men got up to leave, they looked out over Sodom, and Abraham walked along with them to see them off. And the LORD said, "Shall I hide from Abraham what I am about to do? Abraham will surely become a great and powerful nation, and through him, all the nations of the earth will be blessed...."* (Gen 18:16-18). Abraham had reached a level of intimacy in prayer that God considered him to be his servant and friend. Abraham knew the deep secrets of the Kingdom of God. *Where are you in your prayer life and your relationship with God? Are you on fire for God or you have grown lukewarm?*

Apostle James, the brother of our Lord Jesus, a man of prayer himself, speaks eloquently about prayer. Historians like Flavius Josephus who specialized in the history of theology testified that the skin of James's knees was very hard like the skin of a camel, because of the amount of time he spent kneeling in prayer. In a reflection in his pastoral letter, James wrote, "Is anyone among you in trouble? Let them pray. Is anyone happy? Let them sing songs of praise. Is anyone among you sick? Let them call the elders of the church to pray over them and anoint them with oil in the name of the Lord. And the prayer offered in faith will make the sick person well; the Lord will raise them up. If they have sinned, they will be forgiven.
Therefore, confess your sins to each other and pray for each other so that you may be healed. The prayer of a righteous person is powerful and effective.

Elijah was a human being, even as we are. *"He prayed earnestly that it would not rain, and it did not rain on the land for three and a half years. Again, he prayed, and the heavens gave rain, and the earth produced its crops".* (James 5:13-18). What manner of man was Elijah the Tishbite, whose prayer was so incredibly powerful that it shut the heavens for three and half years? Elijah was a man of great faith, authority, and power. A man of unusual anointing and standing. A man who was unwilling to compromise. Listen to what he said to King Ahab, *"Now Elijah the Tishbite from Tishbe in Gilead said to Ahab, "As the LORD, the God of Israel, lives whom I serve, there will be neither dew nor rain in the next few years except at my word."* Watch the words of the Mighty Prophet of God that nothing will happen **"except at my word."**

Such is the demand of one who dares to pray. Real prayer cannot be offered in trifling faith and in the midst of double-mindedness and fear. Real Spiritual prayer must proceed from a heart that is filled with the certainty of one's standing with God. It must also proceed from a heart of certainty that God will respond exactly to the call made according to His will.

Elijah knew that he was certainly one with God. How could he say "except at my word", if he had no faith in what he was saying? Faith is demanded as a base or a foundation of any true prayer. It does not matter who is praying, what matters is this; does the one praying have faith in God? Do they believe that God will certainly respond to their prayer?

Many centuries after Elijah ascended to heaven, Christ taught this aspect of prayer in an amplified and remarkable way as recorded by the gospel of Mark. We see the demand of the imperatives of prayer, *"Have faith in God," Jesus answered;*

"Truly I tell you if anyone says to this mountain, go throw yourself into the sea and does not doubt in their heart, but believes that what they say will happen, it will be done for them. Therefore I tell you, whatever you ask for in prayer, believe that you have received it and it will be yours" (Mark 11:22-25).

In these passages of scripture, the Apostle James and our LORD Jesus Christ offered a deep and profound understanding and teaching on some of the elements that make prayer effective. Here is an exegesis on prayer worth spending years reflecting and meditating on, it is worth studying. You have to study it repeatedly until you discover the spiritual nuggets contained here for your spiritual growth. James says we need prayer when we are in trouble. This sounds basic and elementary.

We all rush to God when we are in trouble. That is common and obvious. It is said we can only understand the value of water when the well is dry. Praying when one is in trouble is common among Christians. But pause and reflect on the second question James asks, "Is anyone happy?" Do you pray when you are happy? Many Christians never take prayer seriously unless they are in trouble. Many Christians pray crisis prayer. Many are prompted to pray when in trouble, but when one is happy and seems to have no pressure, they do not spend considerable time in prayer. But to pray when one has no immediate personal need but praying out of their love for God. This is a different level of prayer. James tells us that it is important whether we are in trouble or are happy to pray. Prayer must be offered not as an event, but as a lifestyle and this is how we ought to cultivate our prayer habits for us to generate effective prayer. When prayer is being offered, one must examine to see if one is in right standing with God. What you do before and after your prayer matters much more than what you are saying in your moment of prayer. *It is the prayer of a righteous man that is powerful and effective.* It is not just any man, but it is a righteous man's prayer that is effective and powerful.

Chapter 2

WITNESSING AND SEEING THE REALITY OF THE POWER OF THE GOSPEL

How do we know that this gospel we are preaching is true? What evidence do we have of the efficacy of the gospel?

When Thomas or Didymus had been told that Jesus Christ had risen from the dead, Thomas one of the twelve refused to believe. The account is recorded in the gospel of John. John 20:25 puts it this way, "So the other disciples told him, 'We have seen the Lord'. But he said to them, 'Unless I see the nail marks in his hands and put my finger where the nails were and put my hands into his side I will not believe.'" Thomas was adamant he would not believe unless he was given proof. Thomas needed practical evidence of the story the disciples were telling him.

Today the world has more doubting Thomases. How do we deal with them? Are we going to just shut down as evil unbelievers? When people did not believe, did Jesus just shut them down and condemn them without offering the authenticity of the gospel? It is important to see first how Jesus dealt with those who doubted who He was, and at times sought to test and trap him.

We will begin perhaps begin with this story of our beloved friend Thomas, whom many theologians have come to characterize as the "Doubting Thomas". How did Jesus deal with Thomas? Did he condemn him as an unbelieving wicked disciple? The Bible records in John 20: 26-27, a most wonderful experience a week after Thomas had disputed that Jesus had risen from the dead, and we will capture this from scripture. "A week later his disciples were in the house again and Thomas was with them. Though the doors were locked Jesus came and stood among them and said, 'Peace be with you!' Then he said to Thomas, 'Put your finger here, see my hands. Reach out your hand and put it into my side, stop doubting and believe.' Thomas said to him, 'My Lord and my God!' Then Jesus said to him, 'Because you have seen me, you have believed, blessed are those who have not seen and yet have believed.'" No doubt we see the magnanimity of our Jesus Christ's character and attitude to humanity. He goes beyond human expectations to save man from the depravity of sin and unbelief. He stooped low, to the level of humanity in his compassion to deal with the unbelief of Thomas.

In the letter to the church in Philippi, Paul reflected this character of Christ. Philippians 2:6-8, "Who, being in the very nature God did not consider equality with God something to be used to his advantage, rather, He made himself nothing by taking the nature of a servant being made in human likeness and being found in appearance as a man He humbled himself by becoming obedient to death, even death on a cross." This is the mind-boggling side of Jesus Christ. He who knew no sin became sin so that He might redeem humanity from the curse of sin. The love Jesus has for humanity although we are sinful, Christ is unwilling that any should perish, but that all should come to the knowledge of God. The word says, "Yet while we were sinners Christ died for us" (Romans 5:8). This is the extent of His incomparable and incomprehensible love for humanity.

Let's look at the story of the unbelieving Samaritan woman as recorded in the book of John, by John, the beloved disciple of Jesus Christ. In John 4: 10.-19, "Jesus answered her, 'If you knew the gift of God and who it is that asks you for a drink, you would have asked him and he would have given you living water.' 'Sir,' the woman said, 'you have nothing to draw with and the well is deep. Where can you get this living water? Are you greater than our father Jacob, who gave us the well and drank from it himself, as did also his sons and his livestock?'" The Samaritan woman did not believe in Jesus Christ: taking Him to be an ordinary and natural man who was making some bizarre claims about himself. As a way to mock Jesus about his claim that he could give her living water, "the Samaritan woman asked, 'Sir, give me this water so that I won't get thirsty and have to keep coming here to draw water.' He told her, 'Go, call your husband and come back.' 'I have no husband,' she replied. Jesus said to her, 'You are right when you say you have no husband. The fact is, you have had five husbands, and the man you now have is not your husband. What you have just said is quite true.' 'Sir,' the woman said, 'I can see that you are a prophet.'"

Jesus had disarmed this woman and made her believe; by exposing the pores in her marital life. Eventually, in John 4:29, she went into the city proclaiming, "Come and see a man who told all I have ever done, could this be the Messiah?" When the people of the city came, what started as the unbelief of one person, became a means of salvation for the whole city. Here in this story, we witness the GOSPEL at WORK, impacting and transforming the lives of many people for the glory of God, and fulfilling the mission and the mandate of our LORD Jesus Christ. At the end of it, we see Jesus telling the woman, "Yet a time is coming and now has come when the true worshippers will worship the Father in Spirit and in truth, for they are the kind of worshippers the Father seeks. God is Spirit and his worshippers must worship in Spirit and in Truth." *(John 4:23)* This statement of Jesus has cut across history and remains one of the most profound teachings the master gave.

In the ninth chapter of the book of Mathew beginning with the second verse, we encounter this story, "Some men brought him a paralyzed man lying on a mat. When Jesus saw their faith, he said to the man, 'Take heart your sins are forgiven.' At this, some teachers of the law said to themselves, 'This fellow is blaspheming!' Knowing their thoughts, Jesus said, 'Why do you entertain evil thoughts in your hearts? Which is easier to say, your sins are forgiven or to say, get up and walk. But I want you to know that the Son of man has authority on earth to forgive sins.' So he said to the paralyzed man, 'Get up take your mat, and go home." Then the man got up and went home'". (Matthew 9:4) Once again, we see Jesus Christ going beyond to offer proof of who He was, by performing this remarkable miracle. It was not just talk, but He proved what He said by what He did. "For the Kingdom of God is not a matter of eating and drinking but righteousness, peace and joy in the Holy Ghost." (Romans 14:17). Paul in 1 Corinthians 2:4, said, "My message and preaching were not with wise and persuasive words but with a demonstration of the Spirit's power, so that your faith might not rest on human wisdom, but on God's power". It was not just a message that someone had put up. The power demonstrated through the message, SHOWED the authenticity of the GOSPEL. The life of Apostle Paul was a remarkable testimony and witness of the transformative power of the Gospel. The first time we meet Paul, he is at the scene of the murder of a prominent Jewish believer Stephen. Paul is not just there; he is consenting to and was part of the plot to kill Stephen by stoning him. Acts 8:1-3, "And Saul approved of their killing him, (Stephen). On that, a great persecution broke out against the church in Jerusalem and all except the apostles were scattered throughout Judea and Samaria. Godly man buried Stephen and mourned deeply for him. But Saul began to destroy the church. Going from house to house, he dragged off both men and women and put them in prison."

Why was this young man Paul so angry? What wrong or evil had the apostles done? What Crime had Stephen committed? The crime Stephen had committed was to tell the Jews the gospel; that Jesus of Nazareth, whom they had crucified was LORD was the expected Messiah whom the nation of Israel had waited for centuries. But the messiah in the form in which Jesus presented himself was anathema to the Jews, how could their reigning messiah be crucified? Surely according to them, Jesus of Nazareth did not fit the description of their expected Messiah. This is what infuriated Paul. The message of the Cross according to Paul then was a fraud and a gangrene that had to be stopped before it spread further. It was a message and teaching that was contrary to Judaism. Act 9:1-6, "Meanwhile Saul was still breathing out murderous threats against the LORD's disciples. He went to the high priest and asked him for letters to the synagogue so that if he found any there who belonged to the Way, whether men or women, he might take them as prisoners to Jerusalem. As he neared Damascus on his journey, suddenly a light from heaven flashed around him. He fell to the ground and heard a voice say to him, 'Saul, Saul why do persecute me?' 'Who are you, Lord?' Saul asked. 'I am Jesus whom you are persecuting,' he replied. 'Now get up and go into the city and you will be told what to do.'"

Paul was determined to destroy and put an end to the church. The church was seen as I have said, as a dangerous sect that was spreading a message contrary to Judaism. Understanding Paul's background; that he was educated under a respected Jewish teacher of the Law, Gamaliel, he naturally felt that he was well equipped to understand the Torah and obligated to defend Judaism. This gave Paul, a sense of pride and esteem. He believed he was part of the cream of Israel, an esteemed Pharisee, and, "though I myself have reasons for such confidence. If someone else thinks they have reasons to put confidence in the flesh, I have more: circumcised on the eighth day of the people of Israel, of the tribe of Benjamin, a Hebrew of Hebrews in regard to the law, a Pharisee as for zeal, persecuting the church, as for righteousness based on the law, faultless" (Philippians 3: 4-6).

How did a man who hated the church so much and all that it stood for become a fearless defender of the GOSPEL? As we look at Paul's life, we see the power of the GOSPEL at work in someone's life. Paul's personal journey started with his dramatic encounter with Jesus on his way to Damascus. Paul was a feared opponent of the church and the early Christian community. Many Christian leaders feared him. In response to God's command to Ananias to go and pray for Paul, Ananias said. "'Lord I have heard many reports about this man and all the harm he has done to your holy people in Jerusalem. And he has come here with authority from the Chief priests to arrest all who call on your name.' But the Lord did not give in to the fear of Ananias. The Lord replied, 'Go! 'this man is my chosen instrument to proclaim my name to Gentiles and their kings and to the people of Israel. I will show him how much he must suffer for my name.'" When Ananias finally laid his hands on Paul and prayed for something dramatic to happen. Apostle Paul, a murderer turned into a fearless preacher of the GOSPEL and the church he tried to destroy.

Years later, Apostle Paul recounted the experience in a letter to the Galatian church. In Galatians 1:21-24, "Then I went to Syria and Cilicia. I was personally unknown to the churches of Judea that are in Christ. They only heard the report: 'that the man, who formerly persecuted us is now preaching the faith, he once tried to destroy.' And they praised God because of me."

No doubt Paul's Spiritual transformation is shocking. It happened in a dramatic way! We hear him saying in Galatians 2:20. "I have been crucified with Christ. It is no longer I who lives, but Christ lives in me. The life I now live in the body, I live by faith in the Son of God, who loved and gave himself for me." It is clear that through his conversion, Paul received a new life in Christ Jesus. This is what he terms "the Life I now live" mean. It signified a new life he had received, he was a new man, a herald, and a torch bearer of the GOSPEL he hated.

It was difficult and unbelievable for many who heard the GOSPEL for the first time. It did not make sense and seemed a far-fetched story. But this is the reality of the power of the GOSPEL. Paul says in 1 Corinthians 1. 18, "For the message of the cross is foolishness to those who are perishing but to us who are being saved, it is the power of God." In the early years of his ministry, Paul did not understand the GOSPEL, he thought the claims being made were foolishness. No wonder he hastily joined those who were stoning Stephen and became an arch-enemy of the church. But when the power of the GOPSEL had touched this hardened Pharisee, his eyes were open. The veil fell off.

Explaining this to the Church in Philippi, he said, "But whatever were gains to me, I now consider loss for the sake of Christ". (Philippians 3:7) How could he consider circumcision, his identity as a Pharisee as dung? How could Paul say, "May I never boast except in the cross of our Lord Jesus Christ, through which
the world has been crucified to me and I to the world. Neither circumcision nor uncircumcision means anything, what counts is the new creation" (Galatians 6:14). Unbelievable to many, how could circumcision mean nothing to a Pharisee? This was the identifying mark as an Israelite, a descendant of Abraham. We can only say that something practically happened to Paul when he encountered the true GOSPEL.

I have a personal testimony to share about the practical power of the GOSPEL of the Cross of Jesus Christ. When I went to law school, because of bad company, I drifted into a life of sin and debauchery. I got engrossed in immorality and alcoholism. I lived a daily life of sin. It had become normal to me. I felt no shame or guilt. My heart and conscience were dead to the core. I mocked those who believed in God. I thought as Marxists say it, "religion is the opium of the poor." I
never knew that there was a vast difference between religion and Faith. Religion seeks to fulfill the rituals and motions of the religion while faith is about building a relationship with God. This is what Christianity is.

I went deeper and deeper into sin. I became an owner of a nightclub called ZIKO in Chitungwiza, Zimbabwe. We did a lot of despicable things at the club that I am not proud to repeat in this book as a born-again Christian. Along the way, I met a lot of compromised preachers. Some of them came to consult me as a lawyer on many issues. I had also become a prominent lawyer in Zimbabwe, being featured on TV and radio every week. Although these pastors tried to witness to me, their lifestyles were questionable, and I had first-hand information on their dodgy lifestyles. It became difficult for me to believe. I judged everyone on the moral standard of these few pastors I had met. I described the church as them and them as the church.

In consultations, in the hope I could help them escape their troubles, they would confess to me in client and attorney confidentiality and ask me for a way out. I was shocked and petrified and this galvanized my view that the church and the whole idea about God was a joke and a fable of incomparable foolishness and ignorance. Yet God has mysterious ways of touching and changing our lives.

One night the LORD supernaturally visited me in a revelation that came through this BIG DREAM that changed my life and this dream has never left me. The angel came to me and took me to a screen and played a video of my life. The angel of the LORD showed me everything that I ever did. Years later, after reading the story of the woman at the well, I understood when she said, "Come and see a man who told me everything I ever did, could be this the messiah? In this dream, the angel of the Lord showed me all I ever did. I heard the voice for the Wages of Sin is death and the gift of God is eternal life. The angel plainly told me that, because of my life of sin, I had no place in the Kingdom of God, and if I were to die like this I would go to hell. I PLEADED with the LORD in desperation and fear, I accepted to surrender my life to Jesus Christ. After weeping for almost three hours, I woke up and I was a new creation in Christ Jesus. My desire for alcohol and immorality was taken away from me on that blessed day. I have been free since!

No man laid his hands on me but God Himself! My life and my zeal for God have never been the same again. I hungered and thirsted after God. I wanted more of God. When the Lord asked me years later to surrender my business and career, although there was a struggle, I finally did. I have not looked back, and neither have I ever regretted being a herald of the GOSPEL. I have found joy in sharing the GOSPEL of the CROSS. As you read this book, your life will never be the same again.

The Christian faith is the only way or "religion", where a man comes down from heaven to die for the sins of humanity. How could this be? But this is exactly what happened with Jesus of Nazareth. Born of the Virgin Mary, Jesus Christ became the means through which the sins of humanity could be atoned for and forgiven. All that happened when Jesus Christ was crucified at the CROSS of CALVARY. He died in reality, he was buried but in reality, he rose from the dead three days later. Through his death and resurrection, those who believed, has received the forgiveness of sins and a new life in Christ.

Chapter 3

THE FOUNDATION OF TRUE PRAYER

"By the grace God has given me, I have laid a foundation as a wise Master Builder and someone else is building on it. But each one should build with care. For no one can lay any other foundation other than the one already laid, which is Jesus Christ. If anyone builds on this foundation using gold, silver, costly stones, wood, hay or straw, their work will be shown for what it is, because the day will bring it to light. It will be revealed by fire, and the fire will test the quality of each man's work" (1 Corinthians 3:10-13). If one wants to build something lasting and meaningful, one needs a sound foundation.

It is absolutely important to understand that "without a solid foundation, you will have trouble creating anything of value." Wisdom demands that "you cannot build a great building on a weak foundation. You must have a solid foundation if you are going to have a strong superstructure" (Gordon B Hinckley). Prayer like a building, needs a solid foundation. What then is the foundation of prayer? The foundation of prayer is the true gospel. If one does not know the true gospel and the true doctrine of Jesus Christ, how can such a person pray effectively?

In my study and my practice of the discipline of prayer, I have come to the understanding after careful reflection, that it is only believers who have a true knowledge of the gospel, had a deep abiding life of prayer. It is possible to pray to a God whom you do not know, but it is impossible to pray effectively to a God whom you do not sincerely and genuinely know.

Prayer without a deep and intimate knowledge of God, is merely religious motions of human repetitions, only gratifying the fleshly desire of the human being. Sometimes the human being is so caught up in religion that he is easily deceived and does not even recognize that he is lost. Jesus's conversation with the women at the well of Samaria reveals the dangers of religious knowledge. The women were so concerned about the observance of the external motions of religion, a mere mental assent that left the heart of the creature untouched and unchanged.

In John 4: 19, the Samaritan woman said, "I can see that you are a prophet". But she rushes to say "Our ancestors worshipped on this mountain, but you Jews claim that the place where we must worship is in Jerusalem." The Samaritans considered Mount Gerizim to be a sacred mountain, where they had to come to meet God. For the Jews, you had to go to Jerusalem, and Mount Moriah was the place where Abraham, the first patriarch of Judaism, nearly sacrificed his son Isaac thousands of years ago. It was on this mountain where the Jews thought it was so important to go and worship. They forgot it was not about religious rituals, but about a man's relationship with God and the state of man's heart. For the Samaritans as long as a Samaritan went to Mount Gerizim, it satisfied their religious quest regardless of what was in their heart. For Jews, it was Mount Moriah. This is what religion does, it centers on religious rituals and motions, but not on the condition of a person's heart or relationship with God.

Jesus makes a remarkable and profound response that has shaken the hearts of religious people for centuries. He ripped open the tomb of the hypocrisy of religion. Therefore, a prayer stimulated by religious zeal and knowledge is a mere enchantment and noise that can not ascend to the throne of God. In Revelation 5: 8, we are told, "And when he had taken the scroll, the four living creatures and the twenty-four elders fell down before the lamb, each holding a harp and a golden bowls full of incense, which are the prayers of the saints."

It is clear that the prayers of the saints that go before the throne of God is like incense, a fragrance, an aroma before our Holy and Mighty God. Jesus's answer left an indelible mark on the theology of the Samaritan woman and eventually changed an entire city. Jesus said, "'Woman,' Jesus replied, 'believe me a time is coming when you will worship the Father neither on this mountain nor in Jerusalem. You Samaritans worship what you do not know, we worship what we do know, for salvation is from the Jews. Yet a time is coming and has now come when the true worshipers will worship the Father in Spirit and in truth, for they
are the king of worshipers the Father seeks. God is Spirit and His worshipers must worship him in Spirit and in truth'" (John 4:22-24). It is these worshipers who are in Spirit and in truth who must offer real and effective prayer to God.

What kind of prayer life do you have as a born-again believer? What kind of a believer are you? Are you truly consecrated unto God? Are you a true Christian? Real and authentic prayer as I have said must be built on a firm and sound foundation. Real and true prayer must born from a deep conviction of the reality of God and his word. God must be ALIVE to us, I mean God is Alive but is he Alive to us? You must then treasure God's word and live in it. You must pay attention to God's word and obey it. In real life storms are going to come, that want to shake our faith. Is our life built on the rock, Jesus Christ, that although storms come through our prayer life and relationship with God we will not be shaken? Jesus warned us in Mathew 7:24-26, "Therefore everyone who hears these words of mine and puts them into practice is like a wise man who built his house on a rock. The rain came down, the streams rose and the wind blew and beat against the house yet it did not fall because it had its foundation on the rock. But everyone who hears these words of mine and does not put them into practice is like a foolish man who built his house on the sand. The rain came down, the streams rose and the winds blew and beat against that house and it fell with a great crash". The reason why the second house fell with a great crash is because it was not built on the rock.

Your Christian life is like a house. On what have you built it? Is your house built on the rock or on the sand? Many Christians remember God when they are in trouble. They pray when trouble comes. Some people easily get discouraged. When storms of life come to test their life, they stumble and fall. When they start to talk to you about their problems you wonder, did they really believe Jesus Christ in the first place? Yes, they did but forgot to add prayer to their life, I mean consistent prayer to anchor their life on. They did not find the joy of reading God's word. I say this to you as long as you are in this world, pray and do not lose hope. Pray and watch so that you may not fall into temptation. Prayer is the weapon God has given you to build and defend your faith in Jesus Christ.

Chapter 4

A RETURN TO THE TRUE GOSPEL: BRINGING CHRIST'S LIFE TO THE CHRISTIAN COMMUNITY IN THE LAST DAYS

Chapter three in this book is perhaps the most important part of my writing and will perhaps remain the most profound contribution I will make in bringing the church back to its husband Jesus Christ. It is important before you start reading this chapter, that you empty your heart of deceitfulness and pollution, the carousing that has filled the world today. In your heart, let there be a new desire, a renewed desire to want the truth without compromising it.

The yearning to embrace the gospel without twisting it to fit into our corrupted human ego. You must be willing to let go of your EGO and allow Jesus Christ to take his rightful place in your life. You cannot want GOD and want it your way. We can't play to the whim of the human flesh and call on the name of God. We can't pursue the idolatry of human fame and call on the name of God. We can't want to read into the bible what we want and call it theology or Christian faith. We can't embrace the philosophy that there are many ways to reach God
when Jesus Christ says, "'I AM the ONLY WAY' to the Father" (John 14:6). Money can buy fame, but money CAN'T buy the TRUTH. If the TRUTH can be presented in so many ways, then it's not the TRUTH. Having listened to an uncompromising savior Jesus Christ, Pilate asked Jesus, "WHAT IS TRUTH?" (John 18:38) You must see TRUTH as a singular noun linguistically and not plural. All truth is true and therefore, there is a singular truth!

Similarly, although there may be perceptively many gods, there is ONLY ONE TRUE GOD. People may claim that God is this and that, in ACTUALITY, ONLY ONE TRUE GOD exists. We live in a world filled with the conundrum of humanism, where the human WILL is competing to establish its own individual
human hegemony. The human WILL controlled by Satanic and demonic manipulation, seeks to establish the human being as master of his own fate. This is an attempt to undermine the AUTHORITY of GOD. Then Satan said, "I will be like GOD."

This is the GREATEST DECEPTION in human history and one that must be countered by strict obedience to the command of the word of God. The ONLY PLACE we can find the TRUTH is in the GOSPEL. In the true GOSPEL, Christ's supremacy and omnipotence is totally revealed. Jesus said, "I AM the WAY, the TRUTH, and the LIFE." Nobody can understand TRUTH without coming into fellowship with Christ. Because Christ himself is the sum total of the TRUTH He says, " IAM THE TRUTH". He is the form and substance of TRUTH.

WHERE DO WE START?

"And this gospel of the Kingdom will be preached in the whole world, as a testimony to all nations and then the end will come." Matthew 24:14. The greatest joy of anyone who is born again, is waiting for the second coming of our Lord Jesus Christ. The second coming of Christ will usher in those who are truly born again, and members of the Kingdom of God; a glorious entry into Christ's eternal glory and reign. Who does not want to be caught up together with him and enter into this eternal glory? How can you be born again and not wait in anticipation of this?

This is what Apostle John, the beloved disciple of Jesus records in the book of Revelation 21:1-4, "Then I saw 'a new heaven and a new earth,' for the first heaven and the first earth had passed away and there was no longer any sea. I saw the Holy City, the New Jerusalem coming down out of heaven from God, prepared as a bride beautifully dressed for her husband. And I heard a loud voice from the throne saying, 'Look! God's dwelling place is now among the people and he will dwell with them. They will be his people, and God himself will be with them and be their God. 'He will wipe every tear from their eyes. There will be no more death or mourning or crying or pain, for the old order of things are gone forever.'"

Apostle Paul in his letter to the Christians in the city of Thessalonica, candidly captures what will happen when the much-awaited second coming of Jesus takes place. Apostle

Paul says to the believers, "For the Lord himself will come down from heaven with a loud command, with the voice of the archangel and with the trumpet call of God and the dead in Christ will rise first. After that, we who are still alive and are left will be caught together with them in the clouds to meet the lord in the air. And so, we will be with the Lord forever" (1 Thessalonians 4:16-17).

In order for us to experience this glorious exit and enter into the marvelous and magnificent reign of Christ, something must happen. This glorious reign of our Lord Jesus Christ will not take place until "the gospel of the Kingdom is preached." The GOSPEL of the Kingdom of God is so important that the END will not take place without it being preached to the whole world. If the gospel is so important, that END times will ONLY come with it being preached, then, the gospel is worth understanding, so that the church would know what to preach and what to concentrate on and help to usher in the second coming of Christ.

This is so radically important, especially in this twenty-first century, where the church and the gospel have come under intense attack from the Kingdom of Satan. Many churches have been polluted and adulterated. The pastors have been seduced by the devil into preaching a counterfeit gospel, which is no real gospel at all, bringing shame to the body of Christ. Christ said he is coming back for a church, "And to present her to himself as a radiant church without stain or wrinkle or any other blemish but holy and blameless" (Ephesians 2:27). Yet today's church is full of blemishes and wrinkles. The church is falling short of the glorious and radiant state Christ is expecting from his church at his second coming. As we search the scriptures, we see that "The ONLY solution to this crisis is the GOSPEL."

The Bible is like a vast sea; if you cast your net, you are likely to catch something. Not everything is a FISH. An experienced fisherman will know what fish to eat and not eat and what fish is fit for human consumption. To avoid this spiritual dilemma, Apostle Paul instructed the young Christian leader, Timothy, "Study to show yourself approved unto God, a workman that need not to be ashamed rightly dividing the word of God" (2 Tim 2:15). It is the duty of every true Christian, to study the word of God daily with utter devotion and loyalty to God, in order to show understanding of what God's will is.

When a believer has been acquainted with the word of God, it is their duty to instruct others accurately in the word of God. This is reflected in the story about Apollos, "Meanwhile a Jew named Apollos, a native of Alexandria came to Ephesus. He was a learned man, with a thorough knowledge of the scriptures, He
had been instructed in the way of the Lord and spoke with great favor, and taught about Jesus accurately, though he knew only the baptism of John. He began to speak boldly in the synagogue. When Priscilla and Aquila heard him, they invited him to their home and explained to him the way of God more adequately."

It seems to me that the apostles spend considerable time teaching the church about the GOSPEL of the Kingdom of God, yet many Christians today don't seem to understand what the GOSPEl actually is or what a preacher ought to focus on in their ministry of the word.

The word GOSPEL simply means good news or glad tidings. The gospel is the good news of who Jesus Christ is and what he has done to rescue humanity from sin. Jesus Christ is the word of God that became flesh. The word of God is the master key for every generation. Indeed, God does nothing without his word. This is so powerful when looking at the creation story in the book of Genesis, "In the beginning was the word and the word was with God and the word was God. The word (Jesus Christ) became flesh And dwelt among us." (John 1:1, 14)

However, there is something about the GOSPEL that is as important as reflected in the scriptures. In the book of Mathew 4:23, we are told that "Jesus went throughout Galilee, teaching in their synagogues, preaching the gospel of the Kingdom, and healing every disease and sickness among the people". Jesus Christ spent his time PREACHING the GOSPEL of the Kingdom of God. His preaching was intentional and deliberate, and the focus was the GOSPEL of the Kingdom of God. Jesus did two things, he taught (TEACHING) to those who are already converted.

Pastors need to know this and I use the term pastor in a generic sense, "You TEACH Believers and you PREACH to unbelievers". This is not so much in today's church. There is religious mumbo jumbo in the church. Much of what we hear is not the GOSPEL but motivational speeches meant to appeal to the emotional needs of the people.

Apostle Paul as I have already said elsewhere in the early pages of this book, had warned Timothy, that he needed to spend his time studying the word of God so that he was able to rightly divide the word and present an accurate GOSPEL to the people. The GOSPEL had to be TRUE. Therefore, in those circumstances understanding the GOSPEL was a critical part of one's ministry in the early church. This was so important to the early apostles.

This is evidenced by how Apostle Paul describes himself in his Epistle to the Romans, "Paul, a servant of Jesus Christ called to be an apostle and SET APART for the GOSPEL of GOD" (Romans 1:1). Paul was saying he was called for a specific purpose that is to preach the GOSPEL of the Kingdom of God. In Romans 1:16-17 Apostle Paul continues. "I am not ashamed of the gospel of Christ for it is the power of God unto salvation to everyone that believes to the Jew first and also to the Greeks. For therein is the righteousness of God revealed from faith to faith as it is written the just shall live by faith." There is a sense of depth and profoundness in these verses. Paul reveals that this GOSPEL of the Kingdom of God was not something to be ashamed of. Paul calls the GOSPEL, the POWER OF GOD UNTO SALVATION.

Why is the GOSPEL the power of God unto salvation? Paul says it so because, "In the GOSPEL (Therein), the righteousness of God is revealed (Romans 1:17). Therefore, in the TRUE GOSPEL, we find or discover the righteousness of God. Jesus Christ and the early apostles did everything and warned the early believers to be vigilant and to protect the GOSPEL from corruption and pollution. Indeed, Christ knew that the false teachers and prophets would come and try to corrupt the gospel. The false prophets and teachers would be so "anointed" and empowered by the devil to try to corrupt the gospel, pollute it, twist it, dilute it, and even mispresent it. The GOSPEL is real life indeed and need not be contaminated. Yet the Illuminati and the New Age agents have devised devious ways of infiltrating the church and presenting a counterfeit gospel.

The dangers of the counterfeit GOSPEL are shown by Jesus Christ in the book of Mathew 24:24, "For there shall arise false Christs, and false prophets and shall show great signs and wonders so that if it were possible they would deceive the Elect."

The battle is so real and raging. Satan is at work, sending his agents into the church, sending wolves in sheep's clothing to undermine the GOSPEL of Christ. The battle to maintain the true GOSPEL has been raging for centuries and with each turn, it seems the devil has tried more and more to distract, deceive, and discredit those entrusted with maintaining the gospel.

The apostle Jude wrote with the wisdom Christ had given him, "Dear friends although I was very eager to write to you about the salvation we share, I felt compelled to write and urge you to contend (to FIGHT FOR) for the faith (GOSPEL) that was once for entrusted to God's holy people. For certain individuals
whose condemnation was written about long ago have secretly slipped among you. They are ungodly people who pervert the grace of God into a license for immorality and deny Jesus Christ our only sovereign and Lord"(Jude 1:3-4). The man of God was encouraging believers of his time that the church, the faith, and the GOSPEL were in grave danger of being perverted by certain people. These people had SLIPPED SECRETLY into the body of Christ. They were the agents
of the devil that Christ had predicted a long time ago, would come and try to deceive and seduce some believers to follow a different gospel. In these circumstances the believers were urged to contend or to fight to maintain the GOSPEL in the form and shape it was given to them by our LORD Jesus Christ. Paul towards the end of his life said, "I have fought a good fight, I have finished the race, and I have kept the faith" (2 Timothy 4:7).

Apostle Paul had to fight a good fight to keep the Gospel he was given from being perverted. He went about his many missionary journeys knowing that the devil was fighting to dilute if not twist the gospel, to undermine its efficacy and authority.

This consciousness was reflected in Apostle Paul's epistles. In his letter to the Galatians, Paul challenged the believers in the city of Galatia.

In Galatians 1:6, he writes "I am astonished that you are so quickly deserting the one who called you to live in the grace of Christ and turning to a DIFFERENT GOSPEL, which is NO GOSPEL at all. Evidently, some people are throwing you into confusion and are trying to PERVERT the GOSPEL OF CHRIST. But even if we or an angel from heaven should preach a gospel other than the one, we preached to you, let them be under God's curse. As we have already said, so now I say again. If anybody is preaching to you a gospel other than what you have accepted, let them be under God's curse." Apostle Paul is adamant that there is ONLY ONE TRUE GOSPEL although many would attempt to preach many kinds of gospels. It is clear that today's church is inundated with many kinds of gospels.

Many believers have been seduced by these perverters and others have been thrown into confusion. As I reflect seriously on what the TRUE GOSPEL is, I can see how serious this problem is and how the church has slipped into error and lawlessness. I am utterly shocked as I listen to what many preachers are preaching in the church of God. Many churches are lost and have slipped into SELF-HELP DOCTRINE and are terming their SELF-HELP IDEAS as the GOSPEL. This is a GOSPEL that is NO GOSPEL at all. Christ and GOD are mentioned here and there but the focus and the intent is not to present Christ or the Gospel of Christ, but to motivate and encourage people. It may sound so well, good and charming, but it is not the gospel. In the third chapter of his letter to the Galatians Apostle Paul shows a great annoyance to the believer's behavior. In Galatians 3:1, the apostle writes, "You foolish Galatians who has bewitched you? Before your very eyes, Jesus Christ was clearly portrayed as crucified." Paul was saying to the church of Galatia, you are acting foolishly. Was it not that when the GOSPEL was first preached to you, it was about the fact that Christ was presented clearly as crucified. The GOSPEL hinged on the fact that Jesus Christ was crucified on the cross of Calvary for our sins, he was buried and rose again on the third day and ascended into heaven. He is at the right hand of God and is LORD. How then are you turning to these other nefarious stories about the gospel of the Kingdom of God? The crucification and resurrection of Jesus is the REALITY of the GOSPEL. No wonder Apostle Paul says in Galatians 6:14, "May I never boast except in the cross of our Lord Jesus Christ through which the world has been crucified to me and I to the world." Paul said of himself, "I have been crucified with Christ, it is no longer I that lives but Christ. The life that I now live I live it by faith in the Son of God who died for me" (Galatians 2:20). This is the truth, the ONLY thing worth boasting about in this life is NOTHING BUT the cross of Jesus Christ.

In another passage, Apostle Paul writing to the church in Corinth said to the believers, "For the message of the cross is foolishness to those who are perishing but to us who are being saved, it is POWER of GOD." The message of the CROSS OF JESUS CHRIST, which is the GOSPEL has power. It is the POWER of GOD. It is also the POWER of GOD unto Salvation. This is the reason why the devil does not want the church to preach the GOSPEL but allow them to preach cleverly devised stories. Go on social media and listen to what is being preached, it is shocking. The church has become a harlot, a Hollywood, an arena of entertainment. The preachers do not want to talk about the cross of Calvary and the second coming of Jesus Christ. One big pastor once said, "People do not want to hear about the cross and about the blood of Jesus or nails. You cannot talk about that in the boardroom when folks are busy trying to figure out how to get jobs". The preacher went on to say the reason why people are suffering is because we are preaching Jesus Christ to them. When I heard that, I screamed; God help us! The church has

lost it. Apostle Peter in 2 Peter 1:1-3 warned the church of such people, "But there will also be false prophets among the people just as there will be false teachers among you who will secretly introduce destructive heresies even denying the sovereign Lord who bought them bringing swift destruction on themselves. Many will bring the way of truth into disrepute. In their greed, these teachers will exploit you with fabricated stories." How much of fabricated stories have we heard in the church today? But these people are bringing SWIFT destruction upon

themselves. God brought swift destruction on this preacher who had mesmerized many people with his heresies God retired him because he was spreading the gangrene and cancer of New Age doctrines. May this be a warning to all of us!

In 2 Peter 1: 16, Peter said. "For we did not follow cleverly devised stories when we told you about the coming of our Lord Jesus Christ in power but we were eyewitness of His majesty." He received honor and glory from God the Father when the voice came to him from the Majestic Glory saying, "This is my son, whom I love with him I am well pleased." The Epistle to the Hebrews warns us in Hebrews 12:1, "Since we are surrounded by so great a cloud of witnesses, let us also lay aside every weight and sin that easily entangles us and let us run with perseverance the race that is set before us, looking unto Jesus the pioneer and perfecter of our faith." If we have to live as we must, we are encouraged to keep

our eyes on the cross of Jesus Christ AND on Christ himself. Jesus Christ was the answer, is the answer now, and will be the answer tomorrow. This is the meaning of Jesus Christ the same yesterday, today, and forever. Never let go of Christ. It may seem foolish as it appeared to some when I gave up my career as a lawyer and my business. It was not an easy thing to do, I did it with tears and I still feed on those tears today. But I have held onto Christ daily. I have fallen short of the glory of God many times in my walk with God, but I have never let Christ go. I tightly hold onto HIM daily. I have never allowed my personal flaws and human limitations to stop me from striving ahead. Like Paul " When I fall I stand up and press toward the mark" (Philippians 3:14). Sometimes I am overwhelmed with my human failures and I say "When I am overwhelmed lead me to the rock that is higher than I" (Psalm 61:2). I see it over and over again. As Paul puts it, "I do not understand what I do. For what I want to do I do not do, but what I hate I do. And if I do what I do not want to do, I agree that the law is good. As it is, it is no longer I myself who do it but it is sin living in me. For I know that good itself does not dwell in, that is in my sinful nature. For I have a desire to do what is good but I cannot carry it out. For I do not do the good I want to but the evil I do not want to do, this I keep on doing. Now if I do what I do not want to do, it is no longer I who do it but sin living in me that does it. So I find a law at work, although I want to do good, evil is right there with me. For in my inner being, I delight in God's law but I have seen another at work in me, waging war against the law of my mind and making me a prisoner of the law of sin at work within me. What a wretched man I am who can rescue me from this body that is subject to death? Thanks be to God, who delivers me through Jesus Christ our Lord" (Romans 7:15-25). I have struggled with my human flesh and desperately wanted to be totally free, lest when I have preached to others I myself am disqualified. I fear to be disqualified. I plead with God every day that God must not reject me. I have realized I cannot win the battle against Satan relying on my own strength or wisdom. I have learned to surrender to God and put on the righteousness of God through Jesus Christ our Lord. When I am weak then in Him I am strong, when I am sinful in Him I am righteous and when I cannot do it in Him I can do all things through Christ who strengthens me. CHRIST is my hope, my joy, and my All in All. Without him I AM NOTHING.

Chapter 5

BUT WHAT IS THE GOSPEL IN A NUTSHELL

In this world where we live, there are certain things we CAN'T do without. James writing to the twelve tribes scattered abroad, concluded by saying "As the body without the Spirit is dead, so faith without deeds is dead" (James 2:26). So, what makes FAITH ALIVE is it deeds or is it works? The gospel is like the HEART in a body; without it the body is DEAD. The Christian Faith is not Living Faith without the GOSPEL, and therefore the gospel must be understood by everyone who does not want to believe in vain. In his classical message to the church in Corinth, Apostle Paul offers us a profound and life-changing message; **the message that has changed the world.** This is the message that confounded King Agrippa, in a very life-changing conversation between him, King Agrippa, and Paul. Although this seems to be a long quotation, it allows us to capture the conversation and let the word of God speak for itself. The word of God needs no defender. **It is the TRUTH.**

"So then, King Agrippa, I was not disobedient to the vision from heaven. First to those in Damascus, then to those in Jerusalem and in all Judea, and then to the Gentiles, I preached that they should repent and turn to God and demonstrate their repentance by their deeds. That is why some Jews seized me in the temple courts and tried to kill me. But God has helped me to this very day; so I stand here and testify to small and great alike. I am saying nothing beyond what the prophets and Moses said would happen— that the Messiah would suffer and, as the first to rise from the dead, would bring the message of light to his own people and to the Gentiles" (Acts 26: 19-23).

"At this point Festus interrupted Paul's defense. 'You are out of your mind, Paul!' he shouted. 'Your great learning is driving you insane.' 'I am not insane, most excellent Festus,' Paul replied. 'What I am saying is true and reasonable. The king is familiar with these things, and I can speak freely to him. I am convinced that none of this has escaped his notice, because it was not done in a corner. King Agrippa, do you believe the prophets? I know you do.' Then Agrippa said to Paul, 'Do you think that in such a short time you can persuade me to be a Christian?' Paul replied, 'Short time or long—I pray to God that not only you but all who are listening to me today may become what I am, except for these chains.'" (Act 26: 19-29)

What a theological discourse! What a message! Paul's grasp of the message of the Cross and his theological articulation is unparalleled in human history. For centuries scholars have debated over this message. But the more scholarly debates they are, the more archaeological studies undertaken, some with the clear intent of disapproving the story of Jesus's death and resurrection. The plot to deny Jesus Christ's death and resurrection is an ancient plot. If it was not important, why did the

Sanhedrin devise this wicked plot as recorded in the synoptic gospels?

In Mathew 28:12, we hear, "While the women were on their way, some of the guards went into the city and reported to the Chief priests everything that had happened. When the chief priests had met with the elders and devised a plan, they gave the soldiers a large some of money telling them, "You are to say His disciples came during the night and stole him away while we are asleep. If this report gets to the governor, we will satisfy him and keep you out of trouble. So, the soldiers took the money and did as they were instructed. And this story has been widely circulated among the Jews to this very day." Why was it so necessary to create this scheme or this story if the resurrection of Jesus Christ was a harmless CLAIM by a man they deemed to be possessed by a demon?

If their CLAIM was true that Jesus Christ was a deceiver, a liar and a demon possessed man, why pay attention to the words and claims of an impostor, if truly Christ was an impostor? Why pay a large sum of money to stop this story. If the story was not true, it would fizzle out and die down with time? But deep down in their heart they knew the resurrection was true. The Sanhedrin knew there was something about Jesus Christ that pointed to his messianic declaration. Their human ego did not want to accept this verifiable truth. But in their deception they tried to make the story about Jesus's resurrection look like a fabricated story. Let's go back in time to see that this story was not a simple issue as the Sanhedrin would want everybody to believe.

Peter and the other apostles replied: "We must obey God rather than human beings! The God of our ancestors raised Jesus from the dead—whom you killed by hanging him on a cross. God exalted him to his own right hand as Prince and Savior that he might bring Israel to repentance and forgive their sins. We are witnesses of these things, and so is the Holy Spirit, whom God has given to those who obey him.

When they heard this, they were furious and wanted to put them to death. But a Pharisee named Gamaliel, a teacher of the law, who was honored by all the people, stood up in the Sanhedrin and ordered that the men be put outside for a little while. Then he addressed the Sanhedrin: "Men of Israel, consider carefully what you intend to do to these men. Some time ago Theudas appeared, claiming to be somebody, and about four hundred men rallied to him. He was killed, all his followers were dispersed, and it all came to nothing. After him, Judas the Galilean appeared in the days of the census and led a band of people in revolt. He too was killed, and all his followers were scattered. Therefore, in the present case I advise you: Leave these men alone! Let them go! For if their purpose or activity is of human origin, it will fail. But if it is from God, you will not be able to stop these men; you will only find yourselves fighting against God." (Acts 5: 29-39)

But if it was true, then as it was and is now today, it was important that they could find a way to silence this message. However, as we have seen over the years, skepticism does not completely suffice in the face of overwhelming evidence. But the story of Jesus Christ's resurrection has spread to the whole world. It has become the center piece of the gospel.

In Paul's letter to the Corinthian church, Paul clearly sets out the message of the GOSPEL. 1Corinthians 15: 1-8, the GOSPEL is defined unequivocally and is laid bare without contradiction or confusion. This fifteenth chapter of Paul's letter to the Corinthian church, requires careful examination and study. Here is the GOPSEL as set out by Paul, "Now brothers and sisters I want to remind you of the gospel I preached to you, which you received and on which you have taken your stand, by this gospel you are saved if you hold firmly to the word I preached to you. Otherwise you have believed in vain. For what I received, I passed on to you as of first importance that Christ died for our sins according to the scriptures and that he appeared to Cephas and then to the twelve. After that, he appeared to more than five hundred of the brothers and sisters at the same time, most of who are still living, though some have fallen asleep. Then he appeared to James, then to all the apostles and at last of all he appeared to me also as to one abnormally born." I don't know how you feel when you are reading those words. To me, these words are like Spirit and life.

This is the heart of the gospel. This is what we must preach to the world, not the SELF HELP doctrine that has captivated the modern believer and has taken him out of the Kingdom of God. The SELF HELP doctrine has suffocated the American church. It has been fed by the Spirit of greed among the false preachers Satan has raised to deceive the ELECT if it were possible. Jesus Christ did not die on the Cross for the heresy we hear today.

Jesus Christ was wounded for our transgression, He was pierced for our iniquities. He took upon himself our punishment that we may receive the forgiveness of sins and receive eternal life. What happened on the CROSS OF CALVARY is the sum total message, which qualifies to be called the GOSPEL. For all had sinned and fallen short of the glory of God (Romans 3:23). Sin had separated man from God. And I want to tell you today in no uncertain terms as you read this book, "that Sin still separate man from God today, unless repentance is sought by a believer." The wages of SIN is DEATH and the gift of GOD is ETERNAL LIFE in CHRIST JESUS (Romans 6:23).

CHRIST became a sin offering for us, the PERFECT PASSOVER LAMB. Once and for all Christ died for our sins and PAID THE PRICE. Once again in Romans 10:9-13; we are told, "If you confess with your mouth that Jesus is Lord and believe in your heart that God raised Him from the dead you will be saved. For it is with your heart that you believe and are justified and it is with your mouth that you confess your faith and are saved." As scripture says; "anyone who believes in Him will never be put to shame, for there is no difference between Jew and Gentile, the same is Lord of all and richly blesses all who call on him. For everyone who calls upon the name of the Lord will be saved." **What a wonderful and life changing message!**

This is the truth; Christ came to SERVE so that through him we might be SAVED. He allowed himself to be crucified as one without power. He allowed himself to be humiliated, as one who could not answer and avenge himself. Yet, when Jesus Christ cried on the cross that, "IT IS FINISHED!" and when HE HAD GIVEN UP HIS SPIRIT, something happened that had never happened in the history of humanity. It was a clear and unequivocal statement of who Jesus Christ was. Without He Himself speaking of whom He was on the cross, yet He spoke without speaking. A clear message without words. He took hold of nature and spoke through it. **Action indeed spoke loud than words!**

Matthew one of the writers of the synoptic gospels recorded this dramatic event; "Then Jesus shouted out again in a loud voice and He gave up His spirit. At that moment the curtain in the sanctuary of the temple was torn into two, from top to bottom. The earth shook and the rocks split." (Mathew

27:50-51). It was that CURTAIN that separated the Holy Place and the Holy of Holies in the Sanctuary that was torn in two. Previously ONLY the selected High Priest could enter there, "THE HOLY OF HOLIES," once a year to offer sacrifices for the sin of the people. BUT on this day, a new way was made through the death of Jesus Christ on the cross.

Jesus is the WAY, the TRUTH, and the LIFE! Jesus is the way through which we now can only access the FATHER. From that day Jesus Christ made it possible for EVERYONE to enter the HOLY OF HOLIES, through the shedding of his blood on the cross. Matthew continues, "And the tombs broke open. The bodies of many holy people who had died were raised to life. They came out of the tombs after Jesus's resurrection and went into the Holy City, and appeared to many people. When the centurion and those with him who were guarding Jesus saw the earthquake and all that had happened, they were terrified and exclaimed, "SURELY HE WAS THE SON OF GOD." So, Jesus did not leave to chance both to those who believed in Him and those who doubted him, **that He was the son of God.** Angel Gabriel had said to Mary his mother, "You shall call his name Emmanuel, which is translated God with us. HE SHALL SAVE HIS PEOPLE FROM SIN." Jesus came for one reason to offer SALVATION to the world.

SALVATION is the greatest miracle. It is SALVATION that we should be seeking earnestly. Our preaching is meaningless if does not lead a person to SALVATION. This is the message the apostles carried to the world. It gave them joy when three thousand souls were added one day to their number and on another day, five thousand. The apostles did not mind about what type of house they lived in or what kind of a car they drove or how much money they had in their bank accounts.

Their concern was how many souls were they bringing to the LORD.

The apostles' hearts were gripped with the life changing message of Christ, "What shall it profit a man to gain the whole world and lose their soul." This message rung hard into their hearts. The apostles did not mind the flogging, the imprisonments, the insults, and persecution. What mattered to them most was this; that **people were finding reconciliation and salvation in God**. The message was more important than their life. When Paul was being discouraged from going to Jerusalem because it was prophesied that he would bound in Jerusalem, he said to the church, "Why are you weeping and breaking my heart? I am not only ready to be bound, but also to die in Jerusalem for the name of the Lord Jesus." When he would not be dissuaded, we gave up and, "The Lord's will be done" (Acts 21:13-14).

This sense of loyalty and commitment was uncommon. Paul understood that, it was required for anyone given a trust to prove faithful to the call and the commission. This is not so with this charlatan group of prosperity "preachers," spiritual harlots, who exchange the glory of the Lord with personal pleasure and greed. The group have distorted, polluted and diluted the message of Christ. But I am deeply convicted and convinced by the prophetic words of Jesus, "I am building my church and the gates of hades will not prevail against it." I am convinced that the Lamb of God, the word of God will prevail against all forms of demonic manipulation by the Kingdom of Satan. Christ has triumphed and prevailed against the principalities and powers and made them a public spectacle. EVEN NOW much more the **WORD OF GOD will prevail.**

Chapter 6

EFFECTIVE PRAYER BY LEARNING TO TRUST GOD

"Prayer without trust is no prayer at all"- Prophet Tom Tirivangani

We all can pray somehow. Many people in the time of Elijah could pray. Even the prophets of Baal "prayed" their own kind of incantation prayer. They even fell into a frenzy praying but the bible says, there was no answer. Elijah prayed also. But the kind of prayer of Elijah was different. Elijah was determined to prove to the whole nation that **Not All Prayers** were Prayer. In order to do this, Elijah arranged a contest. The prayer contest between Elijah and the prophets of Baal was a contest of power and the reality of TRUE PRAYER. How do we know that your prayer is real or that the God to whom you are praying to is the real God? There must be a remarkable difference between true prayer and false prayer. There is a vast difference between carnal prayer and spiritual prayer. In bringing this important subject to reality, I will explore the story of Elijah and the prophets of Baal. Let us see what happened at the contest between Elijah and the prophets of Baal.

This is an incredible comparison of two forms of prayer. Not every prayer is prayer. Prayer is talking to God who has the power to change your situation. Engaging in true spiritual prayer is like electrifying a house. How do we know the electrician has wired the house properly? Is it by the electrician talking? No, the proof is seen when we turn the switch on, if its proper power or the light comes on.

We see this in 1 Kings 18:21-29, "And Elijah came near to all the people and said, 'How long will you go limping between two different opinions? If the Lord is God, follow him; but if Baal, then follow him.' And the people did not answer him a word. Then Elijah said to the people, 'I, even I only, am left a prophet of the Lord, but Baal's prophets are 450 men. Let two bulls be given to us and let them choose one bull for themselves and cut it in pieces and lay it on the wood but put no fire to it. And I will prepare the other bull and lay it on the wood and put no fire to it. And you call upon the name of your god, and I will call upon the name of the Lord, and the God who answers by fire, He is God.' And all the people answered, 'It is well spoken.' Then Elijah said to the prophets of Baal, 'Choose for yourselves one bull and prepare it first, for you are many, and call upon the name of your god, but put no fire to it.' And they took the bull that was given them, and they prepared it and called upon the name of Baal from morning until noon, saying, 'O Baal, answer us!' But there was no voice, and no one answered. And they limped around the altar that they had made. And at noon Elijah mocked those, saying, 'Cry aloud, for he is a god. Either he is musing, or he is relieving himself, or he is on a journey, or perhaps he is asleep and must be awakened.' And they cried aloud and cut themselves after their custom with swords and lances, until the blood gushed out upon them. And as midday passed, they raved on until the time of the offering of the oblation, but there was no voice. No one answered, no one paid attention."

When we are praying, we are talking to God. If we are talking to God, then God must answer our prayers. In Isaiah 59:1, the word of God affirms, "God is not DEAF that he cannot hear you". When you engage in spiritual prayer God is going to hear you and answer you. In Jeremiah 33:3 God says, "Call unto me and I will answer you and show you great and mighty things you did not know". It is clear that God's will in Christ Jesus. is to hear the cry or the prayer of his children. Psalms 2:7-8, "I will proclaim the Lord's decree, He said to me you are my son today I have become your father. Ask me, and I will make the nations your inheritance, the ends of the earth your possession". In this contest Elijah made a challenge to the prophets of Baal. Elijah said we will see whose prayer and whose God is real.

Let's not just talk about prayer, but let's demonstrate and prove which prayer is true spiritual prayer and which prayer is carnal prayer; that is mere intellectual prayer. Elijah put it to the prophets of Baal in a very simple way, "And you call upon the name of your god, and I will call upon the name of the Lord, and the God who answers by fire, he is God" (1 kings 18:24). The prophets of Baal responded to this challenge by offering what they called prayer, "'O Baal, answer us!' But there was no voice, and no one answered. And they limped around the altar that they had made. And at noon Elijah mocked those, saying, 'Cry aloud, for he is a god. Either he is musing, or he is relieving himself, or he is on a journey, or perhaps he is asleep and must be awakened.' And they cried aloud and cut themselves after their custom with swords and lances, until the blood gushed out upon them. And as midday passed, they raved on until the time of the offering of the oblation, but there was no voice. No one answered, no one paid attention". Absolutely no one answered (1 Kings 18:26-29).

This is spiritual shock! When we say sometimes, we are praying, it is no prayer at all. This is just a religious spirit. We are just talking to ourselves. We are making noises before ourselves. Real spiritual prayer elicits a quick response from God, because He is God who loves to hear the prayer of his children. This is reflected in the way Elijah prayed after the prophets of Baal, and at the time of the offering of the oblation, "Elijah the prophet came near and said, 'O Lord, God of Abraham, Isaac, and Israel, let it be known this day that you are God in Israel, and that I am your servant, and that I have done all these things at your word. Answer me, O Lord, answer me, that this people may know that you, O Lord, are God, and that you have turned their hearts back.' Then the fire of the Lord fell and consumed the burnt offering and the wood and the stones and the dust and licked up the water that was in the trench. And when all the people saw it, they fell on their faces and said, 'The Lord, he is God; the Lord, he is God'"(1 Kings 18:36-39).

You have been praying for years and you have not received an answer to your prayer; examine and consider the way you are praying. Is your prayer a mere ritual? Is your prayer spiritual? Spiritual prayers are **effectual and fervent prayers.** It maybe the intent of your heart or your motive that is hindering your prayer. Apostle James capture this in James 4:1-3, "What causes fights and quarrels among you? Don't they come from your desires that battle within you? You desire but do not have, so you kill. You covet but you cannot get what you want, so you quarrel and fight. You do not have because you do not ask God. When you ask, you do not receive, because you ask with wrong motives, that you may spend what you get on your pleasures".

Keep watch over your motive. Prayer can easily be affected by your motive. Your motive can hinder God from hearing your prayer.

What is motive? How do I determine motive? Answer these simple questions: Why are you asking what you are asking? What for? What is the purpose?

The book of James helps us to understand the danger of a wrong motive in prayer. James 4:1-3, "What causes fights and quarrels among you? Don't they come from your desires that battle within you? You desire but you do not have so you kill. You covet but you cannot get what you want, so you quarrel and fight. You do not have because you do not ask God. When you ask, you do not receive because you ask with wrong motives, that you may spend what you get on your pleasures." James makes it loud and clear that when a believer prays, it is important to check his or her motive.

What you are praying for, is it in God's will? When you ask what is in the will of God, God will answer you, "Ask and it will be given to you; seek and you will find; knock and the door will be opened to you. For everyone who asks receives; the one who seeks finds; and to the one who knocks, the door will be opened. "Which of you, if your son asks for bread, will give him a stone? Or if he asks for a fish, will give him a snake? If you, then, though you are evil, know how to give good gifts to your children, how much more will your Father in heaven give good gifts to those who ask him! So, in everything, do to others what you would have them do to you, for this sums up the Law and the Prophets" (Matthew 7:7-12). It is important that our prayer must first submit to the will of God. Prayer outside the will of God is not real prayer. When we are praying before we begin, we must search God's will. God's will can be seen and found in the Holy Scriptures. The bible will show us what is in the will of God. Therefore before you start to pray find your bible and read it, the word of God will direct you. When we are approaching God in prayer, we can do so confidently that he will answer all our prayers. In John 5:14. We hear, "This is the confidence we have in approaching God, that if we ask anything according to his will he hears us. And if we know he hears us, whatever we ask, we know that we have what we asked him". Therefore identifying and locating God's will is perhaps much more important than the prayer itself. Practice to find God's will and he will enjoy answered prayers. I will discuss more of this in the next chapter.

Chapter 7

TRUE PRAYER

True prayer is God's grace inspired by the Spirit of God. Prayer is food for the soul. Prayer revitalizes one's spiritual life. Prayer energizes and connects one to God. When one prays by the inspiration of the Spirit of God one visits heaven, one brings heaven on the earth. It is indeed A Taste of Heaven. Jesus said to his disciples pray like this, "... Let your will be done on the earth as it is in heaven" (Matthew 6:10). True prayer is asking God to do his will, not the will of man. In true prayer, a man lays down his own will and lay hold of God's will. Therefore, true prayer is a man's longing for God to have his way. No matter how noble our will is, **it is only man's will with the imperfections of man.** "Many are the plans of man, but it is the plan of God that prevails" (Proverbs 19:21). When you set to pray ask God to wipe out your own will and fill you with more of His own will.

When we approach God with a longing to fulfil his will, he will hear our prayer. 1 John 5:14-15, Apostle John reminds us, "This is the confidence we have in approaching God that if we ask anything according to his will he hears. And if we know that he hears us; whatever we ask, we know that we have what we asked of him". Therefore before one sets to pray, a wise Christian will first find out what God's will is by studying and meditating in God's word. Do not rush into prayer, take your time and search into the perfect law of liberty, the word of God and discover God's mind concerning your petition. Many people pray but there is only one prayer that God answers. **It is prayer fashioned and molded in his will.** When you submerge your will in God's will you are sure to get a quick response from God.

True prayer also recognizes the worthlessness of man and the worthiness of God. In true prayer, one cast's away pride and clothes himself in humility. When one's heart is saddled with pride, it is sure one is talking to himsel and not to God. In Luke 18, we have two men praying. In verse 11, one man prays thus, "... God I thank you that I am not like other people, robbers, evil doers, adulterers or even like this tax collector I fast twice a week and give a tenth of all I get". This man's prayer was full of his self-worthiness. This kind of prayer cannot reach heaven. In verse 13, we read, but the tax collector stood at a distance. He would not even look up to heaven but beat his breast and said, "God have mercy on me a sinner."

Our Lord Jesus Christ examined the attitude of the two men in their prayer and concluded, "I tell you that this man rather than the other went home justified before God. For all those who exalt themselves will be humbled and those who humble themselves will be exalted"(Luke 18:14). I urge you by the mercies of God that in view of His grace in 2024, never neglect the discipline of prayer mixed with humility. Let your prayer rise up before the throne of God early in the morning. Psalm 5:3 "In the morning O Lord, hear my voice in the morning I lay my needs in front of you and wait." In Psalm 119:147, the psalmist declare "I rise before dawn and cry for help. I have put my hope in your word."

Every genuine born-again Christian must practice waking up early to pray. Call upon God in the quietness and stillness of the morning and you will hear wonderful things from the Lord. Give God your prime time, your undivided attention in the morning. Remember he is waiting for you every morning. He wants to hear your voice exalting His Holy Name. He is waiting to hear you magnifying his name and praising him for his goodness and mercy. In Jeremiah 33:3, God says, "Call unto me and I will answer you and show you mighty and great things you do not know."

In true prayer, one discovers their real value, their true worth. Prayer is a journey of discovery. By persistently praying you will discover things you never knew about your life, things you never knew about your family or your destiny. My teaching on prayer must be a telling experience. Many people will discover the lost treasure in their life, the unknown potential and opportunities Satan had hidden from their eyes, by making them focus on negative things. You will discover a hidden revelation and secret that will turnaround your life, your career, your destiny, your business, your material life, your financial life for the glory of God. As you engage in prayer, remember, **faith**, energizes your prayer, **faith**, quickens your prayer. It's not just prayer, it is the **prayer of faith** that moves God. Faith moves God into Action. If you want to see God in Action in your life, release faith. No matter how big the battle you are facing, faith provokes God. God is yearning to see a believer full of faith!

"Of all the divine graces, the prayer of faith mixed with love has the power to withstand any pressure. Prayer of faith, mixed with love has the power to destroy any stronghold in your life. It has the power to change any situation. Prayer of faith, prompted by love can open any door; it can bring an end to the misery and disappointments, setbacks and failures of many generations. This kind of prayer will cause God to respond in an amazing way (Psalm 102:17, Isaiah 38:4). It is also a kind of prayer that will maintain your integrity when you are under the pressure of sin and temptation. Therefore, do not neglect the prayer of faith mixed with love (James 5:16)". - Prophet Tom Tirivangani

Chapter 8

WORDS OF WISDOM

The word of God has power, real power to those who believe it and practice the word. When we live out the word of God, we activate the hidden strength in the word of God. We receive life by practicing the word of God. It is not merely by believing the word of God that one finds redemption but by acting on the word of God. Those who truly believe in the word of God act upon it to release the hidden power and strength in the word. When you read the word of God, take a deep pause, ponder over what you have read, reflect on it over and over again. See to it that you obey and do what it says. Your blessing is hidden in your obedience to the word of God. Aim to obey the word of God, in that obedience **you** will find comfort and success. The devil is not afraid of Christians who memorize scripture but never obey the word. Apostle James encourages us, "But whoever looks intently into the perfect law that gives freedom and continues in it – not forgetting what they have heard, but by doing it – they will be blessed in what they do" (James 1:25). In Joshua 1:8 we find deep counsel from the word of God, "Keep this book of the law, always on your lips, and meditate on it day and night so that you may be careful to do everything written in it. Then you will be prosperous and successful". God wants to receive the blessing of God by keeping his word. We can only keep the word of God by practicing what is written in there. Make a habit of meditating the word of God and by obeying it. Act upon the word and the word will do wonders for you. I prophesy to you that as you hold onto the word of God your life shall turn around in Jesus name. I declare that you shall become a wonder in Jesus name. I see you moving from glory to glory, from favor in Jesus name. God has set aside a time for you to receive your inheritance. You have waited for your inheritance for a long time. You are convinced that you are ready for that inheritance. This is the time that is set for you to possess that inheritance. The time to hear from God is now on how you are going to receive your inheritance. For some people inheritance means that good job you have been waiting for, that marriage you desired, that business you always wanted to start, that destiny you have always dreamed about. Your inheritance can only be released by Spiritual words. Not words of man, not ideas of man but words from God. The words you are about to hear are from the spirit of God and are full of life to those who receive them, believe them and an act upon them. The words are pregnant with power, Dunamis power of the Holy Ghost to transform your destiny. This is destiny time, it is career time, its marriage time, its business time, its finance time and it is victory time.

This is victory through the words of Christ. The supremacy of His words. Christ never just spoke he spoke words that bring life. *"The words I speak are both Spirit and life,* (John 6: 63).

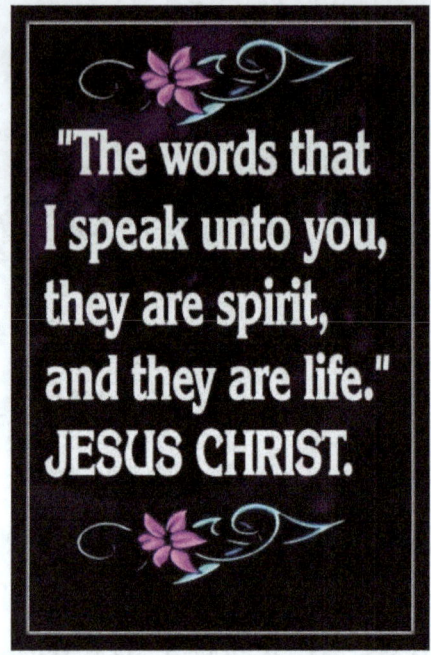

As you read this, pay careful attention to the words contained in this book, they are words inspired by the Spirit of God. These are words that will quicken you and give your life. Jesus said, "I came that they may have life and life more abundantly"(John 10:10). It is only the words of the Holy Spirit that can give your life. The words of the Spirit of God enhance life.

God wants us to mature in our prayer. The aim of our prayer and fasting is that every believer must become mature through prayer, reading the word of God and practicing righteousness "...till we all come to the unity of faith and in the knowledge of the son of GOD and become mature, attaining to the whole measure of the fullness of Christ" (Ephesians 4:13). In order for us to become mature, we must learn to grow in the grace and in the knowledge of our Lord Jesus Christ by practicing righteousness. "But grow in the grace and knowledge of our Lord Jesus Christ. To Him be glory both now and forever. Amen" (2 Peter 3:18).

When we engage in deep sincere and earnest prayer, mediation and reflection, there is now way we can pray and not change, there is also no way we can pray and not mature. Prayer inspired by the Spirit of God and anchored in the word of God causes a believer to grow in maturity as the believer practices prayer and righteousness. In the midst of all this aim to have a pure heart. Our heart is the sanctuary where God dwell. Is your heart true enough, Clean enough, to allow God to establish his throne in it? When we neglect to keep our heart pure and clean we are effectively saying God we do not care whether you are part of our life or not. Prayer that proceeds from a clean heart has tremendous power to change situations and circumstances. It is not so much our lips, it's much more about our hearts. John Bunyan author of Pilgrim's Progress said, "In prayer it is better to have a heart without words than words without a heart". Your heart must be the combustion chamber where prayer must burn, prayer must burn so intense in your heart that Satan cannot come close without feeling the heat from your prayer. Satan cannot stand the heat generated by your prayer. It's so sad that prayer has lost its place in our generation. The believers heart has become cold, very cold that demons find shelter in a born again believer's life. For some, demons have habitation in them in multitudes, legion of demons. If this is your state do not condemn yourself. The real reason is lack of prayer, consistent and persistent prayer makes the demons to flee away. The demons may come to attack but they cannot stay when the believer is burning in prayer. Samuel Chadwick has wisely said, "Satan laughs at our toiling, mocks at our wisdom but trembles when he sees the weakest saint on his knees". Prayer is that weapon that stops and damages the activities of Satan. That is why Satan will do all he can to keep believers from praying. When a believer plans to prayer, Satan will become so jittery that he will do every trick, every scheme to distract you and stop you from praying. He can use anything and anyone around you. The moment you say you want to pray Satan will not let you go scot free. He can use your family and friends to make you lose confidence in what you are doing. When you set to pray know that something will happen to try and stop you. It could be small things and or even big things. No matter what happens to you stick to your plan to pray. Many people prefer to talk about their challenges. In the midst of the challenges, I urge you my brothers and sisters start to pray. Never wait for everything to be perfect. Never wait for a perfect environment. Satan will not allow a perfect environment for you. Keep your focus and keep praying even if Satan wants to make you feel like there is nothing happening. It is the lie of Satan; he wants you to stop praying. He will accuse you of many things, things God has let go in your life. I have learned to keep my prayer in the midst of the storm. If you can learn to pray in an imperfect environment, you have defeated Satan. If he knows you will pray anywhere, he will flee from you. Never allow your environment to stop you from praying.

Chapter 9

UNLOCKING THE SECRET OF A SUCCESSFULL PRAYER LIFE

"He who kneels most stands best" DL MOODY.

It is time for us to reflect on prayer. What has prayer meant to many people in generations past and what does it mean in the future. Take time to think through these precious thoughts on prayer

1. "I have been driven many times to my knees by the overwhelming conviction that I had nowhere else to go. My own wisdom and that of all about me seemed insufficient for the day." -Abraham Lincoln
2. "No man is greater than his prayer life."- Prophet Tom Tirivangani
3. "Prayer is that whole process that reminds us of who God is and who we are."- Mark Lucado

4. "When you affirm big, believe big and pray big, big things happen."- Norman Peale
5. "God shapes the world by prayer. The more praying there is in the world, the better the world will be and the mightier will be the forces against evil." -EM Bounds
6. "Prayer does not fit us for great work, prayer is the great work." -Oswald Chambers
7. "God does amazing works through prayers that seek to extend the grace to others." -Shirley Dobson
8. "When we pray we have linked ourselves to divine purposes and we therefore have divine power for human living." -Stanley Jones
9. "The purpose of prayer is to find God's will and to make that will our prayer." - Catharine Marshall
10. "I have so much to do that I spend hours in prayer before I am able to do it." -John Wesley
11. "He that is never on his knees on earth shall never stand upon his feet in heaven." -Charles Spurgeon
12. "Prayer does not change God it changes me." -CS Lewis

There is no magic formula for a successful prayer life. The scripture offers us an intimate guide and knowledge of what we can do to make prayer effective. The great man and women of God who have been used by God mightily through the centuries testifies to the necessity of prayer. They won souls and nations while on their knees. The stature of their body did not matter as much as the stature and substance of their prayer. At times they were faced with physical threats to their lives but prayer proved mightier than the gun, mightier than an army.

Essential Elements of effective Prayer

"We can do anything we want to do if we stick to it long enough." -Helen Heller.

"Faith sees the invisible believes the unbelievable and receives the impossible" -Corrie ten Boom

Prayer requires persistent seeking and searching and faith to strengthen it. . God wants to answer your prayer when you pray. In Jeremiah 33:3 God says "Call unto me and I will answer you" Our lord desire you to pray to him. He has promised to answer you. In 1 John 5:14, we read, "This is the confidence we have in approaching God that if we ask anything according to his will he hears us". It is very clear from the scripture that God answers prayer made in accordance with his WILL. When we pray it is important that we must ask ourselves if what we are asking God is in his WILL. God and his word are one and God will not respond to anything contrary to his word. As you prepare to pray targeted pray, spend time reading the word of God. The more you read his word, the more you are filled with the knowledge of his Will.

In Mark 11: 22 -25 "Have faith in God Jesus answered. I tell you the truth if any one says to this mountain, go throw yourself into the sea and does not doubt in his heart but believes that whatever he says will happen, it will be done for him. Therefore I tell you whatever you ask for in prayer believe that you have received it and it will be yours. And if you hold anything against anyone forgive him so that your father in heaven may forgive you your sins". Your prayer must therefore be filled with faith and not doubt if God will respond to it. Doubt in a believer's heart offends God. When we are approaching God, it is important to believe him for WHATEVER, or ANYTHING we are asking him. God is not intimidated by whatever you ask him but make sure what you are asking is in his WILL. (In his will means also in his word). Many believers pray for many years and yet have not received an answer to their prayer. Check to see if your heart is pure, is there any bitterness or unforgiveness in your heart. Repent if you want your

prayers to be answered by God. Wrong motives can hinder your prayer life. Here is the biggest trap the devil has laid for the believers. If Satan cannot stop you from praying, he will use his next scheme, he will try to fill your heart with wrong motives. It becomes about you and not about God. By believing in the word of God and allowing flesh to be crucified can out spiritual motivation be radically altered and becomes Christ-ward instead of self-ward. Jesus Christ died for all that they which live should no longer live unto themselves but unto him (2 Cor 5:15). The book of James warns us, "When you ask you do not receive because you ask with wrong motives, that you may spend what you get on your pleasures" (James 4:3). God is interested in knowing what our motivation is in asking for that thing. When our prayer is all about self, be sure God will not answer that kind of prayer. In 2024 let us learn to ask for the comfort of others, for the edification of the body of Christ, for the glory of God. When we pray like this God will also provide whatever we need. God is aware of your needs even before you ask him. God wants his children to have a selfless heart.
In 1 Kings 3:11-13, God said to Solomon "Because you have asked this thing and have not asked for yourself long life nor have you asked riches for yourself nor have you asked for the life of your enemies but have asked for yourself discernment to understand justice, I will give you even the things you have not asked for". It is clear the prayer of Solomon pleased God. Does your prayer please God or please you? Can we see in your asking a motivation to want to please God and obey his word? "And we receive from him whatever we ask because we keep his commandments and do what is pleasing in his sight" (1 John 3:22). We must also aim to continuously practice righteousness. What we learn from the word of God, we must practice and live it out on a day to day basis. Our born-again experience will only make meaning when we live the word of

God. A born-again believer must examine themselves to see if they are still in the faith.

1. Am I a reflection of Christ? Can people see Christ in me without me saying I am a Christian?
2. Am I talking like a person born again?
3. Am I relating with others in the light?
4. Am I following the word of God?
5. Am I glorifying Jesus Christ with my life?
6. What changes have I made to my life since I became born again?
7. Are they new habits I have developed?
8. Can those around me point out to something positive since I received Christ?
9. Am I producing the fruits of the spirit?
10. Am I fruitful in the Kingdom of God?

God wants us to grow in our relationship with him. But how can I grow to be like Christ? I must constantly look at myself and see how far I am from the image of Christ. **Christ is the mirror through which I can look and see my shortcomings.** If I were to look into a mirror and see something wrong, I cannot just walk away. I need to fix it. Similarly when you look into the perfect law of liberty, you will see a reflection of yourself, the word will point out the blemishes and the spots that needs attention. Do not allow shame and embarrassment, condemnation to prevent you from fixing what is wrong in your life. In my quest to have a unique and loving relationship with God I have become intentional. I am not afraid of criticizing myself and say I am wrong here. I am the first person to point out my areas of weakness. I set an immediate agenda to correct it. I am a prophet of my own life.

When you are mature you will recognize that if the holes in your character and attitude are not fixed, it will sink your life. Bad habits no matter how small they are if they are left unattended they will ruin a big destiny. Many great man and women of God have been stopped by their character. They kept sweeping things under the carpet until there was no more room to hide their character flaws and it was too late. They pretended everything was OK but hell was waiting for them. Hell is real, very real to those who practice wickedness. Fear God if you want to spare yourself the torment of hell. Our generation does not want to hear about the realities of hell. The burning brimstone of hell awaits every believer regardless of title, Apostle, Prophet, bishop, who disobeys the word of God. Yes God wants to bless you but not in your sin, not with your bad attitude, certainly not in your anger and jealous. God is holy and he wants you to be holy.

When you are mature you will look at yourself and ask yourself this question, "If God were to bless me in my state of life, where sin and rebellion run amok, what will be the benefit? "Surely what will it profit a man to gain this whole world and lose his soul?" (Mark 8:36) What will a man give in exchange of his soul? When you are mature you can appreciate that it is better to be poor but be a friend of God than to be rich and famous yet an enemy of God. Mature believers hate to take a short cut. Are you in the Lord for many years and do not know how to handle small things? They are many who have spent a long time in the church but are not growing. These are blemishes in the body of Christ. You are in the church for a long time but you are full of pride, you are full of rebellion and disobedience. You are still unreliable and unstable. You do not know where you belong, you belong anywhere and everywhere were THINGS are. Your religion is a religion of Things. You know things more than you know God. I want you to know heaven is a place for those who have forsaken things. Apostle Paul said I choose to know nothing about you except CHRIST crucified and risen. He further said that, that I may know HIM (CHRIST) and the power of his resurrection. JESUS CHRIST himself commanded his disciples, "But first seek eye the Kingdom of God and his righteousness and all these THINGS will be added to you" (Matthew 6:33). When you are mature you know that righteousness is better than riches. The more time you spend in the lord, people must see a reflection of Christ in you. Apostle Paul had a big problem with the believers in the church at Corinth. Although they were in the church for a long time they had not grown into spiritual people. Some of them were acting like worldly people and some of them were like mere infants or childish in the things of God. Paul expected them to have grown in the Lord, but this was not the case. Because they were not growing or maturing the man of God had a problem of how to classify them. It is a disappointment to every teacher to see his students not growing. In 1 Corinthian 3:1, Apostle Paul says, "Brothers I could not talk to you as spiritual people but as worldly people, as mere infants in Christ. I gave you milk, not solid food for you were not ready for it. Indeed you are still not ready". God wants us to increase in our spirituality. He wants us to grow from being selfish to be selfless, from pride to humility, from lies to the truth, from being unreliable to being reliable, from being rebellious to being obedient. God is crying for his children to mature so that they are able to take the Kingdom of God to the ends of the earth. He wants us to mature so that we can receive our inheritance. In Galatians 4:1-2, "What I am saying is that as long as the heir remains a child he is no better from a slave, although he owns the whole estate. The heir is subject to guardians and trustees until the time set by his father". God is calling us to mature so we can receive our inheritance he has prepared for us. God is saying enough is enough, you have had enough time, and you cannot remain a child anymore. It's time for you to receive your inheritance. The WILL has been read. You are a beneficiary; you are nominated to get the inheritance and you cannot play child anymore. Wake up you sluggard Christian. In Corinthians 13:11, Apostle says "When I was a child I talked like a child, I thought like a child, I reasoned like a child. When I became a man, I put the away childish things." It is time for you to put childish ways behind you, anger, malice, jealous, sexual immorality, pride, rebellion, disobedience, envy, competition, gossip, strife, self-promotion, greedy, love of money, idolatry, evil appearance, adultery, because anyone who practice these things cannot qualify to inherit the kingdom of God .

The following are a few key things you need to keep as you pray and fast this year:

1. Have a pure heart
2. Know God's will
3. Have Faith in God
4. Be diligent in your prayer
5. Read the word of God
6. Walking in the Spirit
7. Be selfless

As you say goodbye to the past, make sure you handle your past as a lesson and not as pain. Many people make the mistake of looking at their past as pain and they lose the value of the lesson. If you look at your past as a lesson, you will see how strong you are, how determined you have been, how patient you are and how great your destiny is. I want to exhort you to do two important things as you put prayer into practice. YOU must have an intense hunger to study the word of God. Remember, God is nothing without his word. God and his word are ONE. Therefore **the Word is God** (John 1:1-2). Only a deep thirsting and reverential reading and studying of the Word of God will make you know God better and make you grow in your prayer life. As you grow in your prayer life, your overall spiritual life must reflect this. The aim is this, "that I may know him (Christ) and the power of His Resurrection and the participation in his sufferings, aiming to become like Christ in his death" (Philippians 3:10). If you know Jesus better, your relationship with Him will cause you to grow and mature in every area of life.

It is important that you must learn to pray intensely, allowing the Holy Spirit to teach you how to pray and to allow the Spirit of God to pray through you. Being like Daniel in attitude. Daniel 6: 10, "Three times a day he got down on his knees and prayed, giving thanks to his God as he had done before" (Romans 8:26). We must be active in our way of prayer. Desire that the Word of God and the Spirit of God to interact in your heart. Remember this; it is the spirit that pushes the word of God into action. Faith is perfected when the Holy Spirit prompts us to act on the Word of God. Our ultimate aim is to become a believer who studies the word of God consistently and prays consistently. This is what we call the **UNION OF THE WORD AND THE SPIRIT**. When the Spirit and the word of God are united in your heart you will be able to reach a Spiritual level of growth when as a believer you start producing the fruit of the Spirit. What a joy when you are being fruitful to the Kingdom of God. This is the will of God in Christ Jesus, "that you bear much fruit showing that you are my disciples"(John 15:8). Now come with me to next chapter so I can show how you can do this.

Chapter 10

IMPARTATION OF THE SPIRIT OF PRAYER

The subject of impartation although very important is seldom talked about in the body of Christ. If you ask an average Christian whether they know or have heard or whether they have experienced impartation in their Christian walk, they are likely to say to you, what is that? The body of Christ is suffering because we no longer have preachers that have sufficient spiritual depth required to ensure our generation does not lose its spiritual place in the Kingdom of God. I have observed this in my walk with God when I look at the churches. You see this, one church is good at preaching the Word of God and the Word is given but the Spiritual aspect is neglected. So, it is a word church without the spirit of God. The pastor knows about the word but has scant knowledge about the Spirit let alone the experience of the Spirit. Walking in the Spirit becomes an impossible mountain. Another church is good at teaching about the Spirit. It is a spirit church but very little of the Word of God. This is an unhealthy balance. There must a union of the word and the spirit in order for us to have a living church. Now I have been bringing the word of God to you in the earlier part of this book, but I cannot conclude without talking about the Spirit. As you pay attention prayerfully to this subject of impartation, you are going to experience a spiritual awakening right here as you are reading this book. God has gifted me in this area. Get ready to experience what you have never seen in your life.

I knew very little about impartation until one day when I attended a ZAOGA prayer meeting in the city of Birmingham, West Midlands in the United Kingdom. I had been ordained as an elder in the church and I had a deep hunger for God and more intimately I thirsted for a life of prayer. I felt I was called to be an intercessor. The hunger for prayer burned within me daily but somehow, I felt limited; but I surged forward day and night like a flooded river. I was the odd one out in the church. My joy came when the church said we are going for a prayer meeting. I vividly remember one year my pastor called for a week of prayer and fasting. It was from Monday to Friday. We were expected to fast everyday and break our fast at 6pm with a two hour of prayer, that started from 6pm and ended at 8pm. I started fasting that Monday and went to the place of prayer at 6pm. I was alone because no one else including my pastor who had called for the fast turned up for the prayer. I prayed for the two hours and went home. This happened again on Tuesday, and I prayed for the two hours alone. On Wednesday my father-in-law Bishop Josiah Tarukwasha who had visited us in the United Kingdom joined me for prayer. When we got to the place of prayer called the Jesus center, he was shocked to see that it was only the two of us who had come for prayer. He asked me, "Where is everyone?" I said to him baba, "we are everyone" and I urged him for us to pray and we prayed for two hours. On Thursday this happened again, and I and my father in law prayed for two hours. Late Friday around about 7 pm most of the church members joined the prayer and my pastor came late when we were about to finish. It was a troubling experience for me, but this encouraged me to run the race, knowing the race is a personal one. I knew earlier in my ministry that you cannot serve God while you are looking at others. This is a trap. God wanted me to build a personal relationship with him, he demanded personal loyalty and devotion if he wanted to use me. I could not say God the reason why I am not loyal is because everyone is not loyal. That could not work. Anyway let me go back to what happened in Birmingham. A prayer meeting was called, and we had a guest speaker an apostle from Zimbabwe, a seasoned man of God. As he started teaching on prayer, I sensed an unusual anointing and prompting of the spirit. He was different, he seemed to know much about prayer. After the teaching that lasted for about one and a half hours, he led us into prayer for two hours. I started to watch how he was praying, what he was doing when he was praying. What he was saying when he is praying. I followed him all the way. When he lied down on his tummy, I lied down also. When he knelt down, I knelt down also. When he lifted up his hands, I lifted mine also. This lasted for the two hours and after the prayer meeting, the man of God called everybody together. We were about 150 people. He pointed at me, he said, "Out of everybody in this room, this man is more eager and thirstier for prayer. I have observed him since we started, and I want to pray for an impartation of the Spirit of prayer to come upon him". He prayed for me and commanded that as God had anointed him with the Spirit of prayer that God would fill me with the Spirit of prayer. I felt the presence of God and the blessing of the Spirit. I was overjoyed and I went home fully saturated. This was my real first practical Spiritual experience with the concept of impartation. The day was on Saturday evening.

The following was a Sunday, they called it a Big Sunday. This was when all the branches of the church in the province would gather together for worship. People would come from different assemblies and cities. About 500 people had gathered in the auditorium. The overseer started to lead the prayer, but the atmosphere was so heavy and cold. Out of the fear of embarrassment the Overseer called me and asked me to lead the prayer. At first I felt intimidated but soon gathered my courage. I thought that was God's way of showing me what I had received the previous night. As I started leading the prayer, the congregation was cold, dry, and uncooperative. It was a huge congregation as you could see. However, I never felt discouraged. I felt a renewed sense of the Spirit and continued. Twenty minutes into the prayer, the atmosphere shifted, and the Holy Spirit began to move touching people. Manifestation of deliverances started to happen in the prayer meeting and a breakthrough happened. In unison the 500 people started praying with power and fervently. We were supposed to last an hour, but we went for about 2 hours. Everyone was shocked and asked what happened, they had never felt such a desire to pray. The overseer came to me in utter shock and asked me. "How did you do that elder Tom?" I told him that it had nothing to do with me but that God had taken over; but I knew with certainty it was the prayer of impartation that had radically affected my prayer life overnight. It was clear that something had been deposited into me that night when the man of God laid his hands on me. My prayer life has never been the same since that day. I can lock myself in my office for weeks without going out only praying and reading the word of God. In prayer I remember names and families miraculously as I am urged by the Spirit to pray for them. One by one I pray. Family by family mentioning the members of the family I pray. Even up today I do not know how I can rarely forget people. All I can say. "This is the grace of God that came upon me along with the impartation".

In the book of Romans 1:11-12. Paul says to the believers in Rome. "I long to see you so that I may impart to you some spiritual gifts, to make you strong, that you and I may be mutually encouraged by each other's faith". Paul was eager to impart some spiritual gifts on the church. We may want to ask ourselves, so what is impartation. To impart is to transfer something from one person to another, it is also to deposit something or to be given something or to receive from someone who has more of that thing. Impartation is the spiritual process by which a person who is exceptionally gifted in one area is able supernaturally to transfer and give someone else that gift. Paul as a gifted apostle was endowed with Spiritual gifts and was therefore to transfer what he had to the believers in Rome. In the book of Deuteronomy 34:9. "Now Joshua the son of Nun was filled with the Spirit of Wisdom because Moses had laid his hands on him, so the Israelites listened to him and did what the Lord had commanded Moses." The wisdom that was now operating on Joshua, had come upon him because of the Spiritual act of impartation from Moses. Note, it is written, Joshua had wisdom because Moses had laid his hands upon him. By laying hands upon Joshua Moses had transferred the Spirit of wisdom that was originally in him (Moses) onto Joshua. God had also imparted the Spirit that was upon Moses unto the seventy elders of Israel. Note again it says the "Spirit that was upon Moses". God simply took the Spirit he had originally given to Moses and put the same Spirit upon the seventy elders. In Numbers 11:17, we read, "I will come down and speak with you there and I will take some of the Spirit that is on you and put it on them. They will share the burden of the people with you, so that you will not have to bear it alone". In order for the seventy elders to bear the burden with Moses they had to receive an impartation of the Spirit that was upon Moses, the servant of the Lord. When God has called someone to be a pioneer in one area to carry out God's assignment, when God calls someone for an important assignment, he imparts the Spirit required to carry out the assignment or vision. He then gathers leaders or helpers around the visionary. All the Lord has to do is allow an impartation of the same spirit upon the rest of the leaders. Many Christian leaders do not believe in impartation, or they have very little understanding on what impartation is. No wonder why many churches have divisions because the leaders are competing and are operating in the vision with another Spirit, which is a contrary Spirit. God is not an author of confusion, but Satan is. Many leaders in the church want to be inventors of new things. But the word of God has an answer for us, "What has been will be again, what has been done will be done again, there is nothing new under the sun" (Ecclesiastes 1:9). Solomon, one of the wisest man who has ever lived, gave this advice after a careful study of human life. Yet the church has not fully understood this. Some self-opinionated and arrogant leaders will say I am also called by God. God has also spoken to me. God speaks to everyone. It is true God wants to speak to everyone, but bible history has shown that, God does not speak to everyone in every season or he does not speak the same. They are certain chosen people, God will chose to speak to in a certain special way because He has set them apart for a particular purpose and time. The bible records the story of Miriam and Aaron. In Numbers 12:1, it is written, "Miriam and Aaron began to talk against Moses because of his Cushite wife, for he had married a Cushite. 'Has the Lord spoken only through Moses? They asked. Hasn't he also spoken through us' and the Lord heard this. Now Moses was a very humble man, humble than anyone else on the face if the earth." When God heard this murmuring, he was very angry with Miriam and Aaron. Note that these two leaders were speaking against Moses. They were not speaking about or for, but they were speaking against Moses. They did not realize that once God consecrates someone, God himself comes down to fully inhabit and indwell in that person. When Paul was persecuting the early Christians, Yet Jesus said, "Saul, Saul why are you persecuting me? Paul replied who are you, Lord? Jesus said, I am Jesus whom you are persecuting" (Acts 9.4-5). Have you ever been tempted to speak against your leader because you perceive some kind of error on their part, or you think they want to present themselves like they are the only ones who hear from God? Did you recognize that by speaking against your leader, you may be directly attacking God? Sometimes we do not believe our leaders. You believe they are not good enough and you are better than them. You could actually do a better Job than them. By doing this, sometimes we do not understand that we are speaking against God who set them upon us. We are in actual fact saying, God, you made a mistake to give us a leader like this, you should have given this task to me, I can do it better Lord. Can you actual imagine God making a mistake? Absolutely NO. Yet Many of us one way or the other has fallen into this error over and over again.

To understand why and how serious the talking against Moses by Miriam and Moses was, we will turn back to the story. We are told that God was very angry with the two. He summoned the three of them to the tenant of meeting. God appeared before them in a pillar of cloud and summoned Aaron and Miriam to step forward. God separated the two of them to make sure they understood that he was addressing them, secondly that Moses was separate and different from them. The LORD said, "Listen to my words, when there is a prophet among you, I the LORD reveal myself to them in visions, I speak to them in dreams. But this is not so with my servant Moses, he is faithful in all my house. With him I speak face to face, clearly and not in riddles, he sees then form of the Lord. Why then were not afraid to speak against my servant Moses?" (Numbers 12:6-8). God struck Miriam with leprosy as a sign that this is not acceptable before God. Those of us who are spiritual and acquainted with the Word of the LORD, knows that we must fear to speak against a servant of God. I know in today's church, this is less understood. There is a spirit of familiarity that is overtaken the body of Christ. There is very little or no true fear of servants of God. There is an attempt by the Kingdom of Satan to undermine the authority of man of God and so there is very little desire for true impartation. In Africa where Christians are talking about impartation, there is an adulterated form of impartation. The majority part of it is fleshly work disguised as the work of the Spirit. To write on what's happening in Christian's churches in Africa would require a book on its own. The church has been polluted by charlatans who are masquerading as servants of God. Self-appointed and self-driven pastors, who have no mandate from the LORD but because of greedy and the love of money, they are practicing deceit disguised as the gospel for personal gain. But when we look into the bible we see very powerful testimonies of what impartation can do in the life of a follower or a disciple of Jesus Christ.

After spending some time assisting Elijah, Elisha was confronted with this question by Elijah, "I am about to go, what do you want me to do for you before I am taken from you?" Elisha replied, "I want a double portion of your Spirit"(2 kings 2:9). Notice he said he wanted a double portion of the Spirit of Elijah. Elijah said, "You have asked a hard matter but if you seeing me going, it will be granted to you" (2 kings 2:10). I am paraphrasing the story here. The majority of Christians are familiar with this story. Elisha was tasted and eventually was able to see Elijah go and received a double portion of the Spirit of Elijah. It is remarkable that when the mantle of Elijah fell on Elisha, an impartation took place and it was noticed that the Spirit of Elijah was upon Elisha. What a beautiful story, what an awesome experience. Is this not our generation should be crying for. That no anointed man or women of God should be allowed to die and carry their gifts in the grave, but that spiritual gifts must be transferred from one generation to another. This must be a commitment every Christian leader must have and ensure that the church can grow from one generation to another.

Apostle Paul urged Timothy in his second letter to him that, "For this reason I remind you to fan into flame the gift God which is you through the laying on of my hands" (2 Timothy 1:6). We find a secret here in this verse. Paul was reminding Timothy that when he laid his hands on, he received a gift of God and that it was Timothy's responsibility to fan that gift into flame, that is to make the gift grow. In 1 Timothy 4:14 reminds Timothy again, "Do not neglect your gift, which was given you through prophecy when the body of elders laid their hands on you". Another very interesting aspect emerge here. Timothy had received by impartation another spiritual gift. This time it was when the body of elders had corporately laid hands on Timothy and prophesied a gift into him. Paul seemed very conscious and alert about impartation. You too as a believer can benefit as what happened to Timothy when he was prayed for, gifts were imparted onto him for building the Kingdom of God. Impartation here, is largely done through the laying of hands.

The laying of hands throughout the bible is a practice which is used as a means of contact to confer a blessing or release an impartation from one person to another. The person who is highly anointed or gifted in an area is used by God, where the hands of the highly anointed person becomes a channel or medium through which a gift is transferred from one person to another. It is important to examine this concept of God using the hands of someone in Hebrew. In Hebrew the word hand, which is yadh, is associated with strength, authority and power. This is power which is in the hand, it is therefore noted, and the laying of hands therefore is seen as that which draws from a reservoir of great strength and authority. Hence the ministry of laying on of hands is that which draws from the reservoir of Elohim and is imparted to the recipient. God is the source of the strength, and the impartation can only take place from someone of greater strength or gift in an area to one of less strength. It takes humility to receive impartation. You must recognize a greater gift in someone and look up to that person as a channel through which the gift or anointing will be transferred to you. It is important to recognize that impartation is a spiritual exercise. Therefore, a natural man in himself cannot impart spiritual power, except through counterfeit demonic power from a satanic origin by a person under the power of those influences. The counterfeit is always in inferior in quality and power to the genuine. It is impossible to impart that which you do not personally possess and man does not the power to transmit spiritual power. This dimension is not possible in the natural. So the believer must be spirit filled and must be anointed for the ministry involved. It is a spiritual impartation which not only affects the Spirit of man but both his soul and physical being as well. A new dimension of supernatural spiritual impartation through empowerment by Elohim is given to the Spirit filled believer when he lays hands on another. It can be used to transmit spiritual blessings, giftings, power or authority to the recipient. I believe I have brought you to a place when you understand the concept and process of impartation.

God has highly anointed me in the area of prayer. I have been used by God to transmit the gift of intercessory prayer to others. I have encountered believers who could not pray or utter a single word of prayer transform to an extraordinary intercessor. Many believers have received impartation of the spirit of prayer through my ministry of prayer. Today is your day to receive an impartation that will radically transform your life. Open your heart as I take you through this process and I can assure you that your life will never be the same again. Many people do not understand prayer, or its influence in human life. Some have heard about the power of prayer but few have experienced the real power of prayer. The blessing of a prayer is one of the most profound blessings. No one can ever have a lasting ministry without the blessing of prayer. Prayer can birth new things, prayer can move mountains, and prayer changes everything. Everything is hidden in this, **PRAYER**. You may say I know how to pray. But I want to challenge you, there many levels of prayer. If you really want to change your life stop reading self-help books, stop consulting spirit mediums, stop talking about your problem to everybody. Start to **PRAY**. Jesus was a man of prayer. He rose up early to pray, he secluded himself to pray, and he spent the whole night in pray to God. He said "watch and pray so that you do not fall into temptation, the spirit is willing but the flesh is weak" (Matthew 26:41). He said further that many ought to pray and never give up (Luke 18:1). It is recorded in Hebrews 5:7, "During the days of Jesus's life on earth, he offered up prayers and petitions with fervent cries and tears to the one who could save him from death and he was heard because of reverent submission". There is no shadow of doubt what PRAYER was to our LORD Jesus Christ. Does prayer mean the same thing to you today? How much of your life is given to prayer?

NOW RECEIVE THE IMPARTATION OF THE SPIRIT OF PRAYER

As you come to the end of reading this book I want to give you a blessing, the impartation of the Spirit of prayer. Just believe and open your heart to God as your prayer along with me,

Lord Jesus, I thank you today for the gift of prayer in Jesus's name

Lord Jesus, Prayer is taking to God who has the power to change everything and today I desire to talk to him in Jesus's name

Lord Jesus Christ, son of God , I pray that today you fill me with the Spirit of prayer as you did to Elijah , Moses , Paul and many of your servants. Impart your Spirit of prayer in Jesus's name.

Lord Jesus, I RECEIVE the Spirit of prayer and from today my prayer life will never be same in Jesus's name. If you have prayed this prayer believe and it is Amen, Amen and Amen.

www.ingramcontent.com/pod-product-compliance
Lightning Source LLC
Chambersburg PA
CBHW071025080526
44587CB00015B/2501